Alicia Noors

Understanding
OpenSCAD

A hands-on introduction to OpenSCAD

for 3D printing and CNC milling

FSC

www.fsc.org

MIX

Papier aus ver-
antwortungsvollen
Quellen
Paper from
responsible sources

FSC® C105338

PREFACE

After having been dealing with 3D printing for some time, I have inevitably gained some experience with CAD systems.

As a person keen to experiment, I looked at many software solutions for this.

In addition to the "usual suspects" like Fusion360 or Solidworks, I have found an extraordinary, free, and very practical program.

At first glance, the way OpenSCAD works might seem a bit strange, but anyone who has worked through the first few chapters of this book will quickly see for themselves the flexibility that results from this way of working.

Join me on an exciting journey into the world of OpenSCAD.

IMPRINT

Bibliographic information from the German National Library:

The German National Library lists this publication in the German National Bibliography; detailed bibliographic data are available on the Internet at http://dnb.d-nb.de.

Production and publishing:
BoD – Books on Demand, Norderstedt

ISBN:
978-3752685602

TABLE OF CONTENTS

Imprint..**5**
Preface **5**

SECTION 1 - INSTALLATION & BASICS

Download and Installation...**10**
Windows...10
Mac OSX 11
Linux..12
User-Interface **14**
Stumbling blocks **18**
Representation during rendering / preview...18
Calculation error in object subtraction 20
Basic syntax rules 21
Primitive 2D objects..**22**
Collaboration with other CAD solutions 26
Bring 2D objects into 3D space 27
Units, not mm, cm or inch! 29
Primitive 3D objects..**30**
Combine objects...**34**
Modify objects..**38**
Modifiers...**44**
Variables **46**
Special variables 47

SECTION 2 - PRACTICAL EXAMPLES

Modules..**52**
Loops **62**
Functions **64**
Text...**70**
multmatrix **74**
Multmatrix in detail..78
TWIST **80**
Working with DXF-files..**82**
Working with STL-files...**86**
Check accuracy of fit 88

SECTION 3 - WORKFLOW FROM THE IDEA TO THE FINNISHED PRODUCT

A component gets created..**92**
Preparation & design-concept 92
Design in OpenSCAD...94
STL-Export...96
Slicing for 3D-printing 97
DXF Export for CNC milling 98

Little helpers **100**
MCAD - A OpenSCAD module collection 103

Book recommandations..**104**

SECTION 1

INSTALLATION & BASICS

```
linear_extrude(5)
polygon([[0,0], [0,10], [14,0]]);
```

DOWNLOAD AND INSTALLATION

Windows and Mac OSX users can download the installer or disk image from `http://www.openscad.org/downloads.html`.

Make sure that you do not download the development snapshots. Development snapshots are unstable beta versions that contain the latest features but are only intended for testing purposes. I would strongly advise against the productive use of these versions!

WINDOWS

Download the Windows installer from the URL mentioned above. You can choose between 32- and 64-bit. If you don't know whether you have a 32- or 64-bit system, just try the 64-bit variant, and if it doesn't work, use 32-bit.

In the first step, the installer asks you in which folder you want to install the program.

Normally you can simply accept the suggested value here and then start the installation by clicking on the `Install` button.

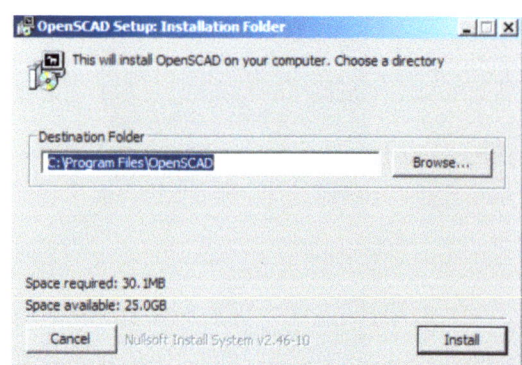

As soon as the installation is complete, you can exit the installer by clicking the `Close` button.

An entry for OpenSCAD was added to your start menu during the installation.

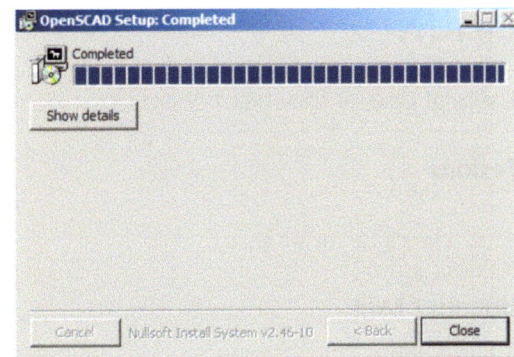

The alternatively offered zip files contain the program including all additionally required files in a folder.

This is particularly suitable if you always want to have OpenSCAD with you on a USB stick. Simply unzip the zip file in the desired location and start OpenSCAD.exe file from that folder.

MAC OSX

After downloading the DMG file, open it with a double click.

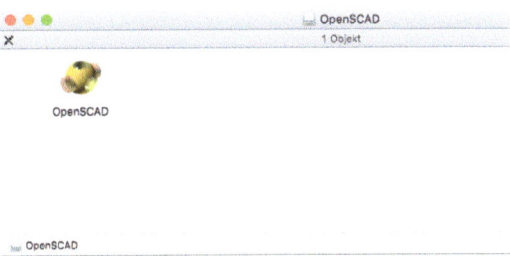

The window shown on the left should then open up.

Simply copy the program into the Applications folder using Finder.

LINUX

Users of one of the mentioned Linux distributions can install OpenSCAD as follows:

Fedora

```
dnf install openscad
```

Ubuntu / Mint

```
apt install openscad
```

Debian

```
apt-get install openscad
```

CentOS

If you use the EPEL repository you can install OpenSCAD with
```
yum install openscad
```

Other Linux distributions

Many other distributions also include OpenSCAD. Therefore try to look for it in your package manager first. If OpenSCAD is not included in the repositories of your distribution, you can build the program from the source code:

Detailed instructions for that can be found at:

```
https://en.wikibooks.org/wiki/OpenSCAD_User_Manual/Building_on_Linux/
UNIX
```

USER-INTERFACE

As soon as you start OpenSCAD you will be greeted by a window that gives you access to your latest projects and the supplied examples.

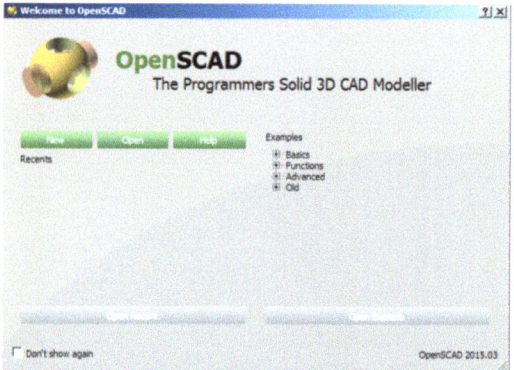

At the lower-left end of this dialog, you can check a box if you do not want to see this welcome screen at startup.

The main window is divided into three areas, which we will discuss one by one ...

Editor

```
1  //circle(12);
2  //circle(d=24);
3  //square(12);
4  //square([12, 6]);
5
6  //linear_extrude(5)
7  //rotate_extrude()
8  polygon([[0,0],[0,10],[14,0]]);
9
```

1

Ansicht: Verschiebung = [0.10 -0.55 0.21], Rotation = [70.40 0.00 30.10], Abstand = 4

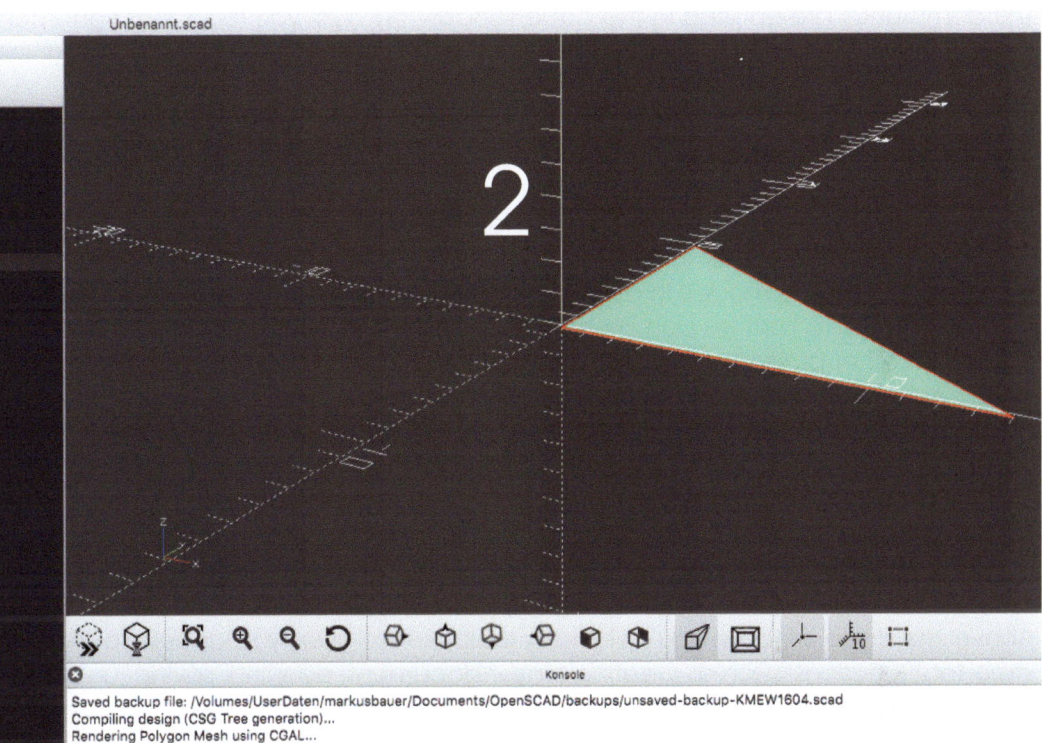

Unbenannt.scad

2

Konsole

Saved backup file: /Volumes/UserDaten/markusbauer/Documents/OpenSCAD/backups/unsaved-backup-KMEW1604.scad
Compiling design (CSG Tree generation)...
Rendering Polygon Mesh using CGAL...
Geometries in cache: 112
Geometry cache size in bytes: 466936
CGAL Polyhedrons in cache: 89
CGAL cache size in bytes: 89046576
Total rendering time: 0 hours, 0 minutes, 0 seconds
  Top level object is a 2D object:
  Contours: 1
Rendering finished.

3

OpenSCAD 2015.03

The commands are entered in the code window (**1**). Yes, you read that right, commands! In contrast to other CAD solutions, models are not designed with the mouse, but with the help of a simple "programming language".

This has several advantages

- Since the language only requires a few commands to describe the models, OpenSCAD is very easy to learn
- By describing the models in a simple language, they can be parameterized very well and entire libraries can be built very easily with your objects, which can be used in other projects
- This results in an extremely high degree of flexibility
- OpenSCAD has been around for a long time and therefore a large community has developed to help you with problems. There are many forums, Facebook groups, and various other channels that you can use to find help.
- There is also a large number of code fragments on the Internet that you can simply copy & paste into your projects and / or modify for your projects.

Above the code window, you will find a toolbar that gives you access to the most important functions, such as creating a new document, opening, saving, undoing or repeating steps, rendering of a model preview or final model for the export as well as exporting an STL file and direct 3D printing over octoprint.

In the preview window (**2**) get the preview of the model and the final rendering displayed.

In this window you can rotate a model in 3D space with the left mouse button, zoom with the mouse wheel and pan with the right mouse button.

You can load any file from the `File` -> `Examples` menu and try this once. Anyone who knows other 3D programs will get along with that immediately. Everyone else will get used to it after a short time!

Below you will find a bar with buttons for standard actions, such as zooming in and out, the standard views left, right, top, bottom, front and back as well as functions to bring the entire model into the visible area with one click or to reset the view if you lose your orientation in 3D space.

If you want to export a PNG image, the exact image section that you see in the preview area is exported in exactly the size of the area. For this, it can also be practical to switch off the coordinate axis or the axis dimensioning, otherwise, these will also be visible in the image.

The console (**3**) informs you about errors in the code. You can also generate status messages yourself in the code, which output gets displayed there, for example, to check the results of calculations.

STUMBLING BLOCKS

OpenSCAD has a few small "peculiarities" that I want to address before we start. If you know from the beginning how the program behaves in certain situations, it will be much easier to get started.

REPRESENTATION DURING RENDERING / PREVIEW

Whenever you save the document, a quick preview is rendered by default.

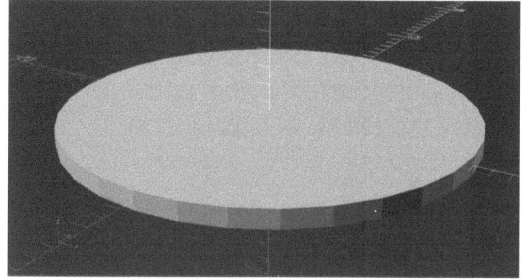

The object shown on the right is not a cylinder, but a circle that can be created with the command `circle(12);`. In the preview, a 2D object is always displayed as a 3D object.

As soon as you render the drawing, a correct 2D representation is used.

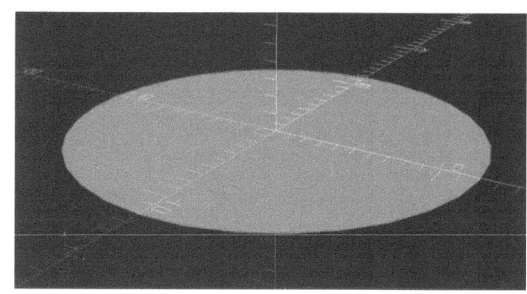

This behavior is mainly because the calculation should be as simple and quick as possible during the preview.

This display error is also related to this. Especially with "holes" that are punched out of an object. This model, which only consists of intersecting flat cylinders, takes this effect to the extreme!

Once the model has been properly rendered, these artifacts will disappear.

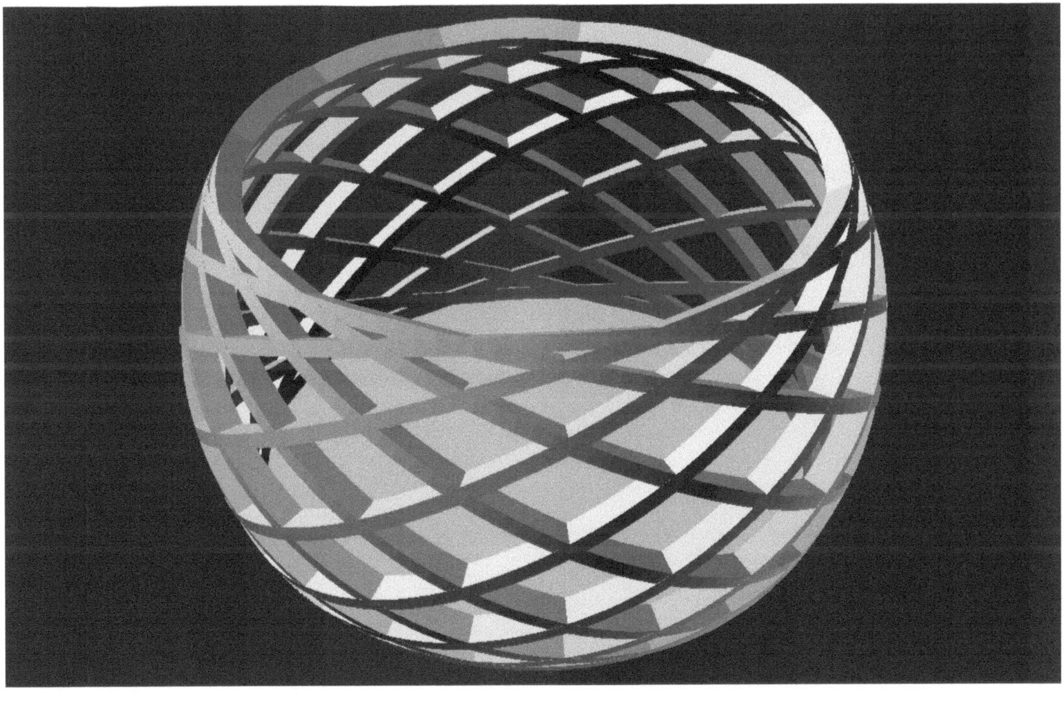

CALCULATION ERROR IN OBJECT SUBTRACTION

On some models, I found such rendering errors in the exported STL files.

Here an attempt was made to punch the cylinder out of the cuboid. If the lower or upper edges are exactly on the same level, a calculation error occurs in some cases that leaves small residues.

So here this hole is not round but flattened on one side, which is not intended in the model.

Please get used right from the start to make bodies that are subtracted from another at least a little longer so that they protrude on both sides.

In this case, I have fixed that error with the help of the `transform`-modifier. Usually, the problem only shows up during the STL export.

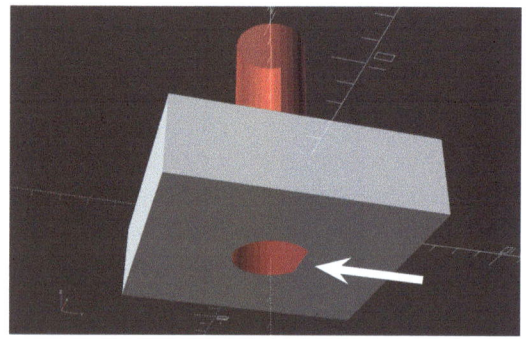

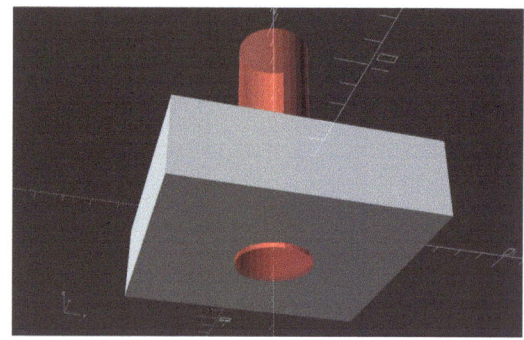

BASIC SYNTAX RULES

The syntax of a programming language is a set of rules according to which well-formed ("syntactically correct") expressions, formulas or program texts are formed from a basic set of characters.

Some rules also apply to OpenSCAD:

Each statement must be terminated with a ;. Therefore, multiple line expressions are created with the ; only at the end of the last line.

```
// One multiline expression
rotate_extrude()
translate([0,10,5])
import(file="test.dxf");
```

Comments are introduced with //. Everything after the // up to the end of the line is ignored by OpenSCAD and only serves as a note for you.

```
// THIS VALUE WAS CHANGED!!!
//circle(17);     Before 21.07.18
circle(17.5); // Since  21.07.18
square(12);
```

Decimals numbers are written in English notation with a point as decimal separator!

```
square(12.7); // so!
square(12,7); // not so!
```

Instructions which define the start of a block end with a { and not with a ;! The block is then ended with }.

```
translate([0,10,5]) union(){
    circle(17.5);
    square(12);
}
```

For a better overview, instructions should be indented within a block. (*Indenting is not needed for syntactical correctness but it makes the code much easier to read for you!*)

PRIMITIVE 2D OBJECTS

In OpenSCAD, more complex shapes are assembled from a set of primitive shapes. This applies to both 2D and 3D models.

Circle

A circle is created with the command `circle`. The specification of a number applies as the radius - for example:
`circle(12);`

The parameter `r` for radius can also be specified explicitly:
`circle(r = 12);`

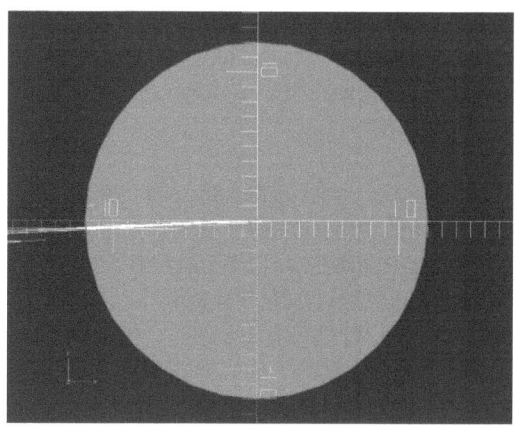

Alternatively, the diameter of the circle can be specified with parameter `d`.
`circle(d = 24);`

All three variants above will create a circle of the same size.

Square and rectangle

Squares are created with the `square` command. Entering a number corresponds to the length of the side - for example:

`square(12);`

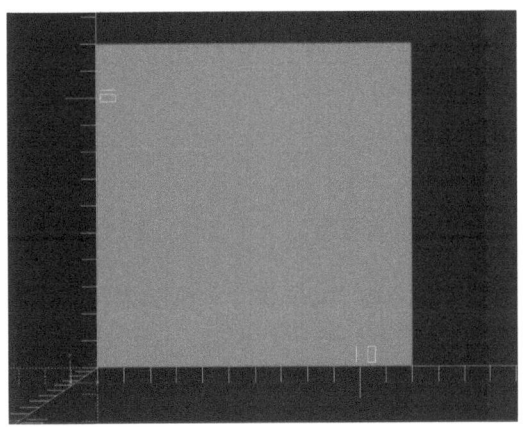

To keep the instruction set as small as possible, the `square` instruction was also reused for the creation of rectangles.

It is not linguistically correct to describe a rectangle as a square, but that is one of the little things that you just have to remember.

By specifying a vector with the X and Y length, a rectangle is created as follows:

`square([12, 6]);`

The first number is for the X-length and the second number for the Y-length.

By specifying `center = true`, the shape will not be created with the lower-left corner point at position `0, 0`, but with its center point (*like the circle*).

Polygon

Any shape with at least three corner points can be created with the `polygon` command.

A list of vectors is passed to this command - for example:
`polygon([[0.0], [0.10], [14.0]]);`

Alternatively, the command can also be written more clearly:

```
polygon([
    [0,0],   // Point 0
    [0,10],  // Point 1
    [14,0]   // Point 2
]);
```

The list is enclosed herewith `[]` and contains vectors (eg `[0,0]`) that are separated from another by commas.

Within the vectors, the X and Y coordinates are precisely in this order.

The shape is automatically closed by connecting the last point straight with the first point, which explains why the 0.0 coordinate is only included once in the list.

Text

Texts can be created with the `text` command. For example, you can specify a font and the size for the text as follows:
```
text("OpenSCAD", font = "Arial",
size = 3);
```

The specification of the font size is based on the units in OpenSCAD.

Of course, the text command offers a few more options like the other commands. However, the aim of the book should not be to present a translation of the documentation. Instead, after a brief introduction, I want to show you practical examples and teach you how to use the strengths of OpenSCAD.

For all less common options of the individual commands, I refer to the very detailed and good documentation:

```
http://www.openscad.org/cheatsheet/
```

COLLABORATION WITH OTHER CAD SOLUTIONS

The construction of complex 2D shapes with the polygon command requires a lot of imagination or a template from which the coordinates can be taken.

Mathematically representable things, such as a star, which can be defined by an outer and inner diameter, as well as the number of spikes, can also be created with the help of loops and corresponding calculations.

Everything else is a bit cumbersome. It is also quite possible that you are working with someone who creates 2D construction drawings in another program and that you only have to prepare them for 3D printing, for example.

Therefore exist the possibility to load a DXF file with the `import` command:
`import(file = "test.dxf");`

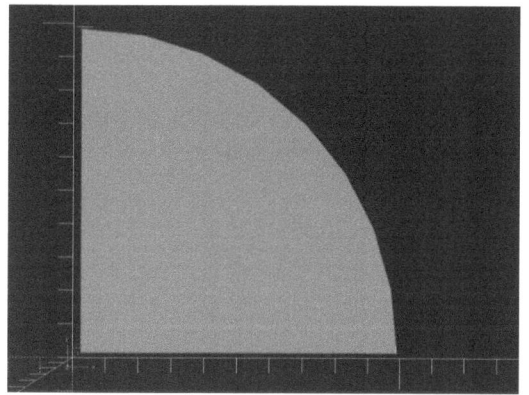

Here, dimensions can be taken and / or only individual layers of the DXF-file can be imported.

3D objects can also be imported from STL or OBJ files.

We will learn more about working with DXF files in the chapter `"Practical example DXF files"`. For a complete list of supported file formats, please see the OpenSCAD documentation.

BRING 2D OBJECTS INTO 3D SPACE

Although OpenSCAD can work with 2D shapes, it lacks important functions, such as dimensions, to produce 2D construction drawings. But that's not really what this program is designed for!

Of course, you could create 2D drawings, export them as DXF files and dimension them in another CAD program, and in exceptional cases, this may even make sense. If you are for example interested in creating 2D shapes for CNC milling without the need of printing construction drawings with dimensioning OpenSCAD can handle that task without a problem. The strengths of this software, however, lie in the 3D area and the flexible creation of 3D models. So let's take a look at how we create 3D model from 2D drawing ...

With the command `linear_extrude` our polygon can be extruded by a certain number of units in the Z-direction - for example:

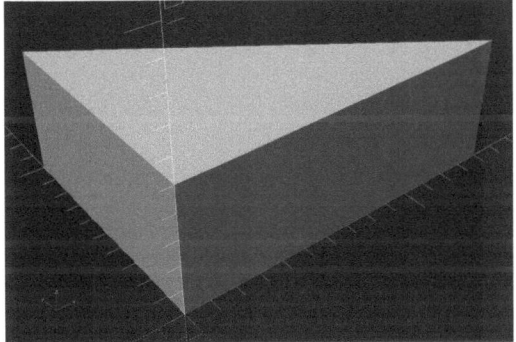

```
linear_extrude(5)
polygon([[0.0], [0.10], [14.0]]);
```

Another possibility to transform a 2D shape into a 3D object is the `rotate_extrude` command.

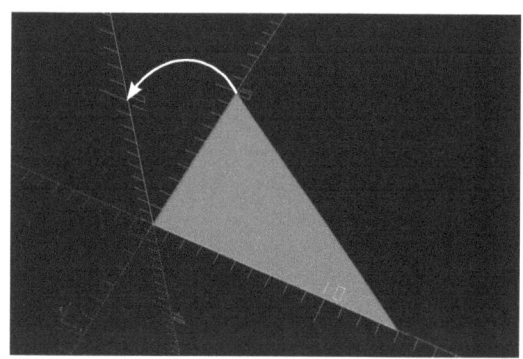

Hereby the shape is fixed on the X-axis and the Y-axis is rotated by 90 ° so that it becomes the Z-axis.

Basically, you can think of it as a sheet of paper that lies flat on a table in front of you and it then simply "stand up".

Then the drawing is rotated around the Z-axis like a gyro - for example:

```
rotate_extrude()
polygon([[0.0], [0.10], [14.0]]);
```

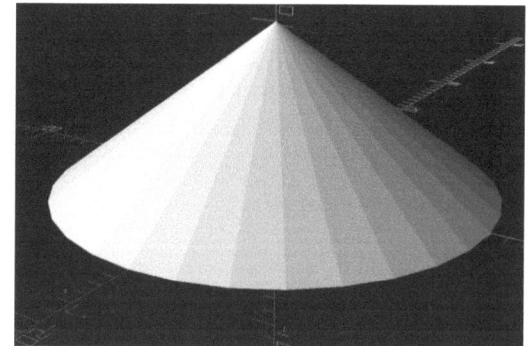

UNITS, NOT MM, CM OR INCH!

As you may have noticed while reading, I never speak of mm, cm, or other units of measurement such as inches. That's because OpenSCAD just doesn't know anything like that.

You design your models in OpenSCAD units of length, and during export, unless absolutely necessary, no unit is defined. If a unit is necessary, 1 unit is exported as one default-unit of the system so mm in a metric system and inch on a non-metric system.

For you, this means that it is up to you to communicate whether the units have to be interpreted as mm, cm, m, inches, light years, Sumerian She or as Klingons qeli'qam.

In practice, it simply means that the step of defining a unit of measurement is eliminated. Programs such as Slicer or other CAD tools will simply use the preferred unit of measurement for the region, depending on which country you are in or which country you have selected in the region settings of the operating system. Models that you open on a german system are interpreted in mm, and models that are loaded on an English system are interpreted in inches.

So unless you're working with an international team, you can just forget about it. For example, if you want to create a model with inches on a german system, you can simply enlarge the model by a factor of 25.4 in the slicer or use a function to calculate the correct dimensions!

PRIMITIVE 3D OBJECTS

Cube or cuboid

Cubes and cuboids can be created with the `cube` command, so the same story as with the `square` command. To create a cuboid use e.g. `cube ([10, 6, 2]);`. A vector is specified for the expansion in the X, Y and Z directions.

And `cube(10);` would simply make a cube with sides of 10 units in length.

Cylinder and cone

A cylinder is defined by the parameters `d` for diameter or `r` for radius and `h` for height:

```
cylinder(r = 5, h = 5);
cylinder(d = 10, h = 5);
```

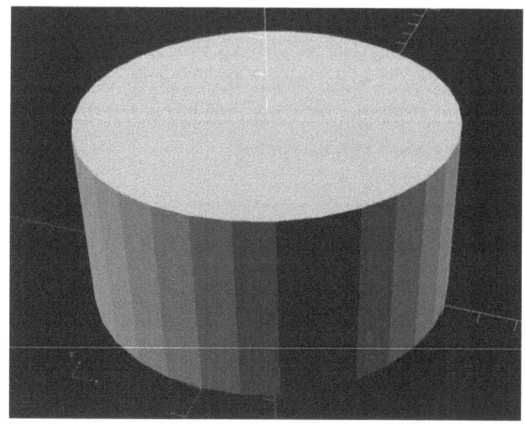

The two commands shown above create identical objects.

In 3D space, the cylinder also has a second task - with d_1 and d_2 or r_1 and r_2, two different diameters or radii can be defined to create a cone.

If you omit d_2 or r_2, the upper diameter is automatically 2 units - eg:
```
cylinder(r1 = 5, h = 5);
```

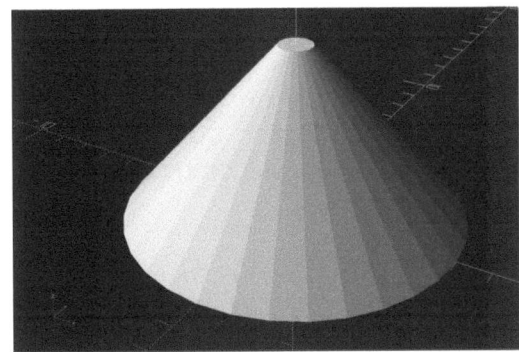

Sphere

A sphere is created with the `sphere` command - for example:
```
sphere(5);
sphere(r = 5);
sphere(d = 10);
```

The notations given above produce the same model. If not specified, the number is interpreted as a radius, of course, you can also specify r for radius or, as with all other round objects, the parameter d specify the diameter.

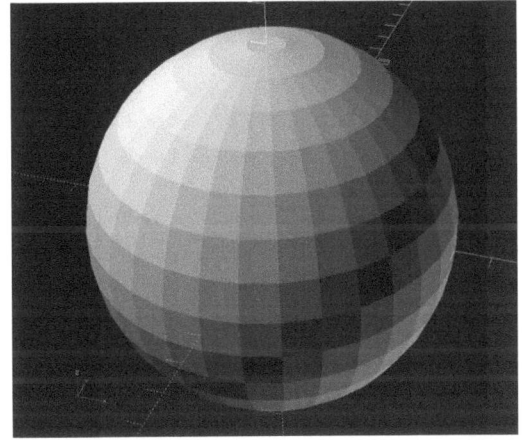

Polyhedron

As with the `polygon` command in 2D space, a polyhedron can be created with the `polyhedron` command:

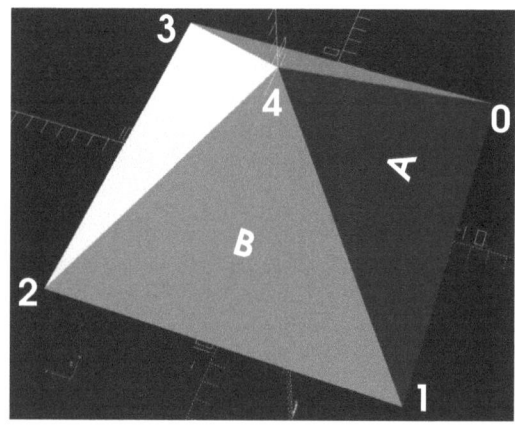

```
polyhedron(
  points=[
    [10,10,0],    // Point 0
    [10,-10,0],   // Point 1
    [-10,-10,0],  // Point 2
    [-10,10,0],   // Point 3
    [0,0,10]      // Point 4
  ],
  faces=[
    [0,1,4],      // Site A
    [1,2,4],      // Site B
    [2,3,4],      // ...
    [3,0,4],
    [1,0,3],      // Bottom half
    [2,1,3]       // Bottom half
  ]
);
```

A list of the corner points is defined with `points = [...]`. As you surely guess correctly, the X, Y and Z coordinates for each point are defined as vectors in this list and the 3D vectors get separated with commas.

The 2nd list (`faces = [...]`) is a list of the points which we definded before, each forming one side.

Side A is the area between corner points 0, 1 and 4. Side B is the area between corner points 1, 2 and 4, etc.

Just draw the missing faces in your head and imagine how you create that pyramid and you will understand the way how that command work!

You could also define the bottom as a square of 4 points instad of using 2 triangles for the bottom:

```
faces=[
    [4,1,2],      // Site A
    [4,2,3],      // Site B
    [4,3,0],      // ...
    [4,0,1],
    [1,0,3,2]     // Bottom square
]
```

There is no need to build all faces with the same amount of coordinates!

Important:
Name the points defining a face clockwise when looking at each face from outside inward. As you see in the example above it's not important with which face or coordinate you start as long as you keep the clockwise order!

Otherwise, it's not guaranteed that the polyhedron is solidly filled.

COMBINE OBJECTS

To create more complex objects, it is necessary to assemble them from the primitive objects you know till now. The following methods of combining are available:

Combine

The `union` command is the standard method for the combination of objects and is also used if you do not specify a method - for example:

```
union(){
    cube(size=[20,20,3],
        center=true);
    cylinder(d=3, h=10);
}
```

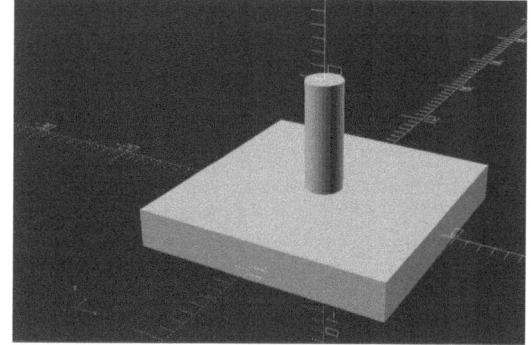

Cutoff

The `difference` command represents the exact opposite - the first object in the block is the basic object and each subsequent object is subtracted from the first object - e.g.:

```
difference(){
    cube(size=[20,20,3],
        center=true);
    cylinder(d=3, h=10);
}
```

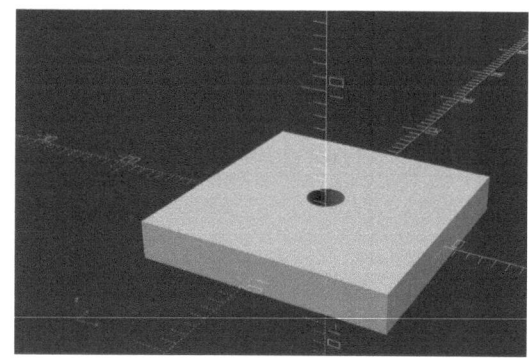

Intersection

The logical third variant would be to create a intersection - for example:

```
intersection(){
    cube(size=[20,20,3],
        center=true);
    cylinder(d=3, h=10);
}
```

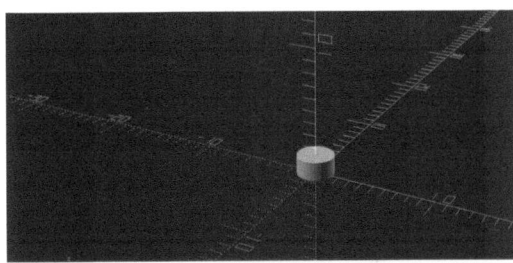

Here the intersection of all objects is formed - e.g.:

```
intersection(){
    cube(size=[20,20,3],
        center=true);
    cylinder(d=3, h=10);
    translate([1,1,0])
        cylinder(d=3, h=10);
}
```

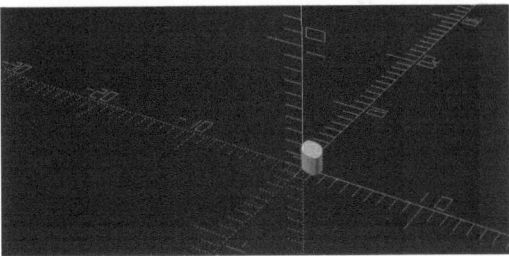

If only one object does not intersect with all the others, the intersection would be nothing and no object is created at all.

In such cases the !, * and # modifiers, about which we talk in one of the following chapters, become very important.

Hull

In order to simplify some constructions a bit, the following two calculation methods have been added. The `hull` function encloses all objects in the block with a shell - e.g.:

```
hull(){
    cube(size=[20,20,3],
          center=true);
    cylinder(d=3, h=10);
}
```

Gaps are hereby also enclosed as you see in the sample ...

Minkowski

To explain this command in more detail, let's take a look at how it works with a 2D example ...

Let's take our polygon triangle:

```
polygon([[0.0], [0.10], [14.0]]);
```

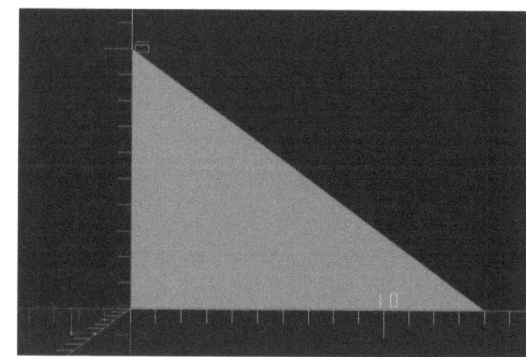

Then we add another object like `circle(r=1);`.

If the 2nd object in the `minkowski`-block would be outside the first object, the first object is moved onto the 2nd one. The object with which the calculation takes place remains in the position where you place it.

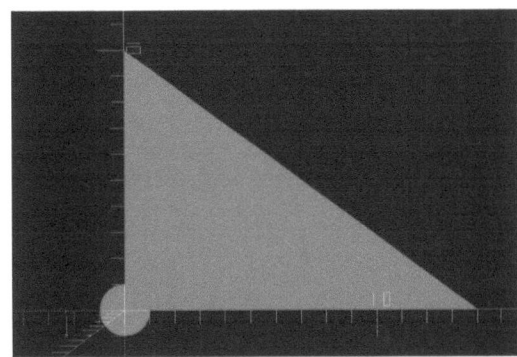

Afterward, the 2nd object is moved around the edges of the previous object and the previous object is expanded.

Here, for example, the triangle has grown for the radius of the circle and it has now round corners. This then forms an intermediate object, which is handled in the same way if another object should be in the `minkowski`-block.

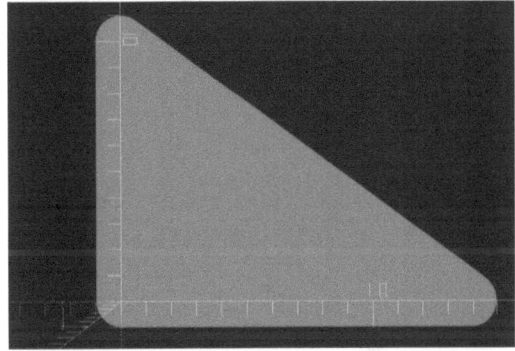

In our previous example, the block becomes larger, higher and has rounded corners with the radius of the cylinder:

```
minkowski(){
    cube(size=[20,20,3],
        center=true);
    cylinder(d=3, h=10);
}
```

MODIFY OBJECTS

Now that you know how to create and combine objects, let's take a look at how we can continue to work with them:

Move

Objects can be moved with the `translate` command. This command takes a vector with the offset in the X, Y and Z direction as a parameter.

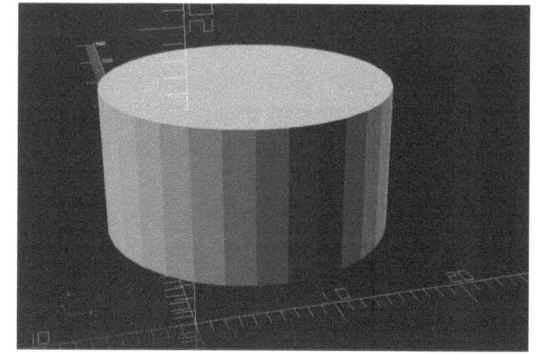

The values are the number of units by which the body should be moved. e.g.:
```
translate([5,5,5])
cylinder(r = 10, h = 10);
```

Rotate

A vector with degree values is passed to the `rotate` command. The values apply to the X, Y and Z axes in exactly this order - for example:
```
rotate([0,45,0])
cylinder(r = 10, h = 10);
```

... to rotate 45° over the Y-axis.

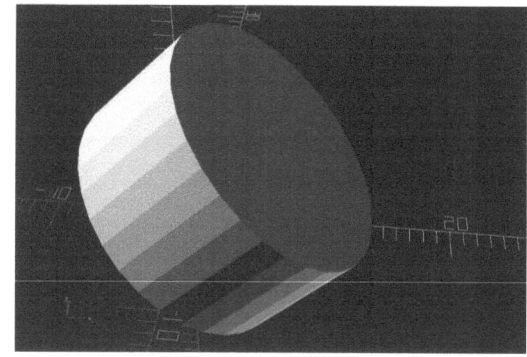

Scaling

The `scale` command expects a list of factors for the X, Y and Z directions in this order - for example:

```
scale([2,1,0.5])
cylinder(r = 10, h = 10);
```

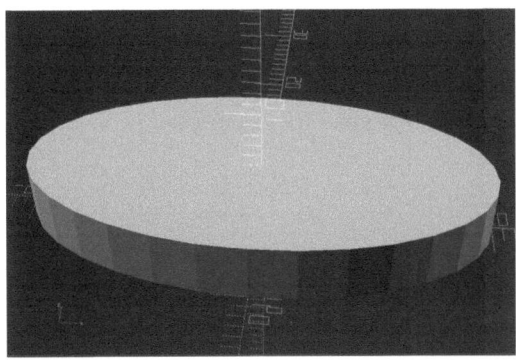

Here, for example, the expansion in X-direction multiplied by a factor of 2 (*200% of the original value*). The 1 in the Y direction does not cause any change and the 0.5 in the Z direction set the height to 50% of the original value.

Resizing

As an alternative to `scale`, resize await the new size in units for the X, Y and Z dimensions:

```
resize([15,5,8])
cylinder(r = 10, h = 10);
```

The cylinder is brought here to 15 units in the X direction, 5 in the Y direction and 8 units in the Z direction.

This is where the difference lies - `scale` works with percentages and `resize` with units of length.

Mirroring

When mirroring with the `mirror` command, a list of booleans (*yes / no values*) is expected. A 0 means no and a 1 stand for yes - for example:
```
mirror([0,0,1])
cylinder(r=10, h=10);
```

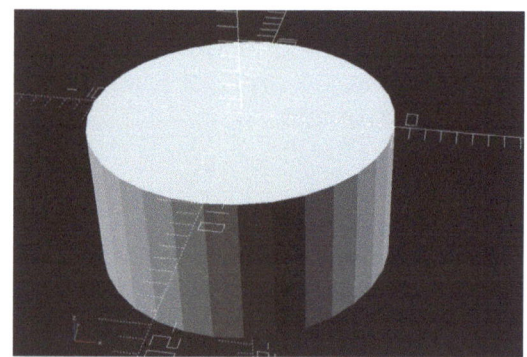

Mirror along the X-axis? No!
Mirror along the Y-axis? No!
Mirror along the Z-axis? Yes!

Colouring

The `color` command only affects the preview and is ignored during exporting! The command expects a list of color values for red, green and blue followed by one value for opacity:
```
color([1, 0.5, 0, 0.45])
cylinder(r=10, h=10);
```

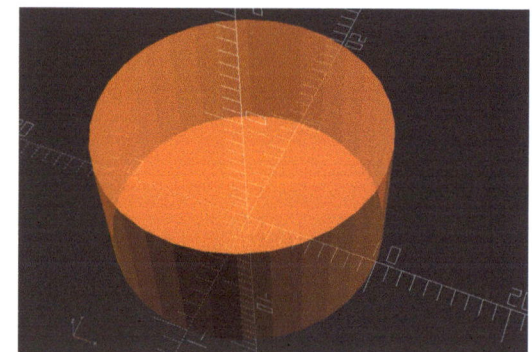

The 1 stands for 100%. That for these values mean 100% red, 50% green, 0% blue and 45% opacity.

Some colors can also be addressed with a name. Therefore you could write the command as follows:
```
color("orange", alpha=0.45)
```

Expand / Shrink

The offset command only works with 2D shapes. Here, the parameter r ensures that the shape is enlarged with a positive value and corners are rounded with a radius of r - for example:

```
offset(r=2)
square([15, 10]);
```

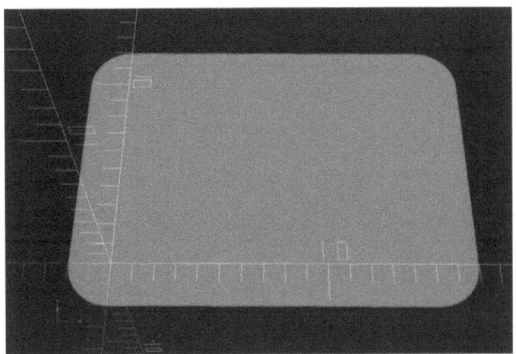

r is also the default parameter - so the following line would mean the same:

```
offset(2)
```

Negative values reduce the shape along the edges. The parameter delta ensures that the forum is reduced or enlarged by the value of delta, but the corners are retained:

```
offset(delta=-1)
square([15, 10]);
```

All the other commands from before also work in 2D space. In that case you have to provide only vectors with X and Y values.

Stretch and tilt in 3D space

The `multmatrix` command looks a bit intimidating at first glance, but is relatively easy to understand once you've played it through - for example:

```
multmatrix([
 [ 1, 1, 10, 0 ],
 [ 0, 2.5, 0, 3 ],
 [ 0, 0, 6, 0 ],
 [ 0, 0, 0, 1 ]
]) cube(1);
```

Diese Matrix besteht aus vier Zeilen mit je vier Spalten. Die oberen drei Zeilen bedeuten folgendes:

X-axis: Scaling factor	X-axis: Shear along Y-axis	X-axis: Shear along Z-axis	X-axis: Offset in units
Y-axis: Shear along X-axis	Y-axis: Scaling factor	Y-axis: Shear along Z-axis	Y-axis: Offset in units
Z-axis: Shear along X-axis	Z-axis: Shear along Y-axis	Z-axis: Scaling factor	Z-axis: Offset in units

The fourth line has no function in OpenSCAD and should always be `[0, 0, 0, 1]`. With this knowledge, we can now analyze what happens to our cube ...

The X-axis (first line):
- 1 for the X-scaling means no size change
- 1 for the shear along the Y-axis in the X-direction ensures that the lower edge of the cube (*near the X-axis*) is fixed and the upper edge of the cube (*further away from the X-axis*) is moved 1 unit in the X-direction. So the edge shears by one unit along the X-axis.

- 10 for the shear of the Z-axis in the X-direction fixes the bottom of the cube and moves the top by 10 units in the X-direction.
- 0 for the offset means that the object remains in its original position.

In the Y-axis (*second line*) there is no shearing of the X-axis (0), scaling along the Y-axis by a factor of 2.5, whereby the cube becomes a rectangle, also no shearing of the Z-axis (0) , but an offset of 3 units along the Y-axis which moves the object in the Y-axis away from the starting-point 0, 0, 0.

In the Z-axis (*third line*) there is neither shearing of the X- nor the Y-axis (0, 0), but scaling in Z-direction to 6 times the height and 0 units offset.

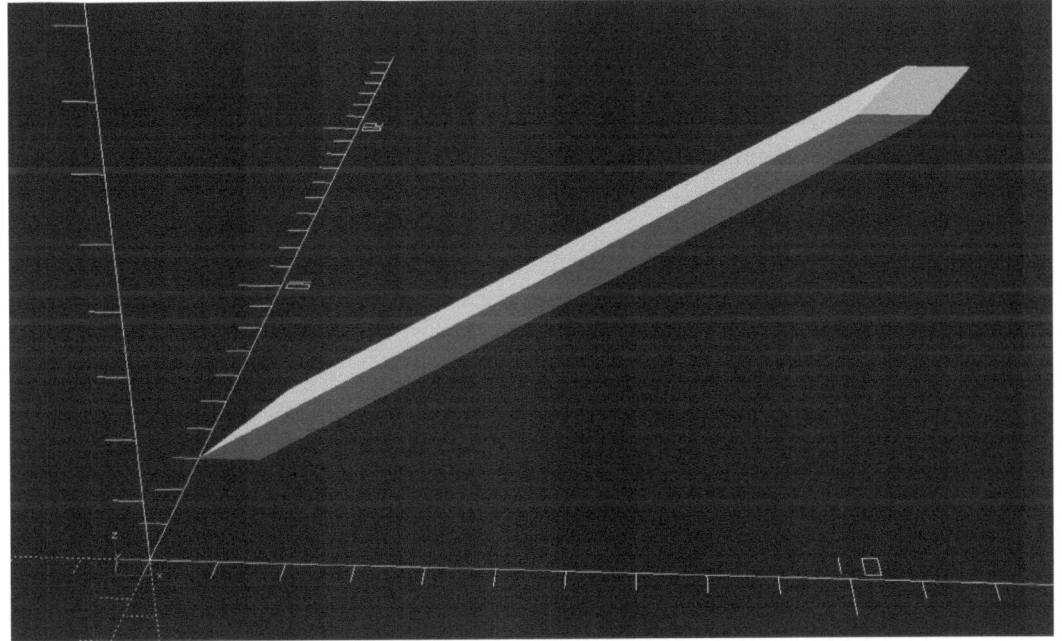

MODIFIERS

When working on models, you may want to check whether the instruction to which you want to make changes relates to the correct part, or that you want to temporarily hide interfering parts.

With the #, the result of an instruction or a whole block is colored in red and displayed semi-transparent:

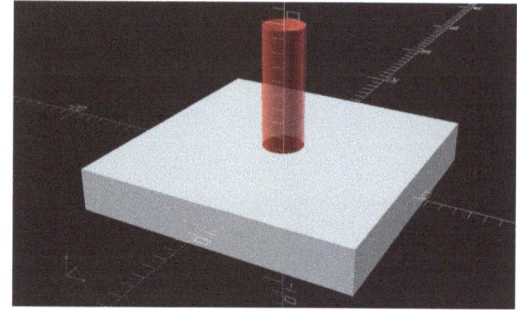

```
difference(){
    cube([10, 10, 3],
        center=true);
    #translate([0,0,-1.7])
        cylinder(d=3, h=10);
}
```

The # is synonymous with `color("red", alpha = 0.5)` but can be written much shorter.

Alternatively, you can also use % to display the object in a semi-transparent gray color. Most of the time, however, the red coloring of # is much easier to see and therefore I never actually use %.

The modifiers # and % only affect the preview, but not the rendering result. One of the reasons for this is that many export formats, such as STL, do not support colors or transparency.

An instruction or an entire block can be deactivated with *-sign:

```
difference(){
    cube([10, 10, 3],
        center=true);
    *translate([0,0,-1.7])
      cylinder(d=3, h=10);
}
```

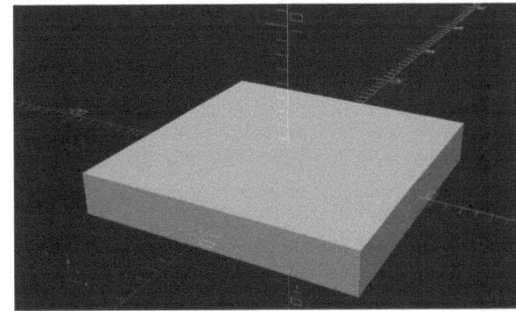

The opposite can be achieved with !. Everything else except this instruction or this block will be hidden:

```
difference(){
    cube([10, 10, 3],
        center=true);
    !translate([0,0,-1.7])
      cylinder(d=3, h=10);
}
```

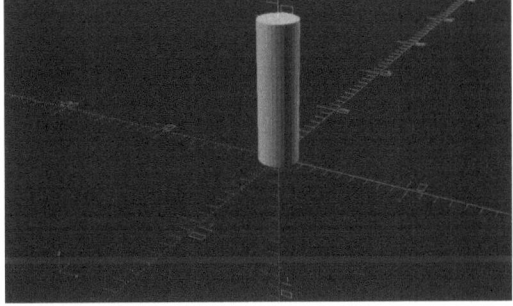

This is particularly useful if you work on a part of the model and want to deactivate all other parts for the moment.

The * and ! affect also the rendering result. So if you just want to export a specific part of a model or everything except one specific part then use that 2 modifiers.

VARIABLES

Variables are used to store values and function as a synonym for the stored value. For example, you can define the values at the beginning of the model and then change all parameters at a central point:

```
length = 15;
width = 8;
thickness = 2;
hole_diameter = 2;

difference() {
    cube([length, width, thickness]);
    translate([length/2, width/2, -1])
      cylinder(d=hole_diameter, h=thickness + 2);
}
```

As you can see, it is much easier to have all the important values for the design in one central place in the code, instead of scattered everywhere. With this four-line long model we don't have a problem with clarity, but when models get longer, changing values directly in the code is usually prone to errors.

You should also get used to giving variables meaningful names. The variable names l, w, t, d would save you some typing, but are you sure that in two or three months you will still know what that abbreviations mean? And what if you would end up in a huge model with t1 till t12, w1 till w12, d1 till d7, etc. Still sure you will know what they all mean in a couple of months?

If I don't follow my own rules of meaningful variable names here in the book it is just for the reason of saving space. So don't do that in your code please!

SPECIAL VARIABLES

OpenSCAD also has some predefined variables - the first group we will look at has an impact on the render quality and thus also on the render speed ...

$fn - number of faces

Faces are the planes of which a body is built of. Faces are also used to approximate a curve. The more of these planes are used, the more time-consuming the rendering and the more precise the curves are.

The number of faces can be determined by setting the variable $fn. By setting this value in the file, the value applies to all bodies - for example:
```
$fn = 12;
cylinder(d=10, h=5);
```

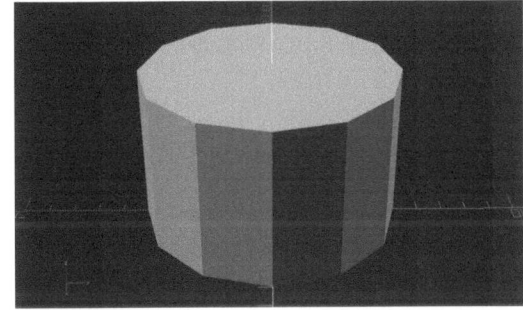

If the value occurs several times in the file, it is always overwritten and the last entry applies.

A higher value resolves roundings more finely - e.g.:
```
$fn = 128;
cylinder(d=10, h=5);
```

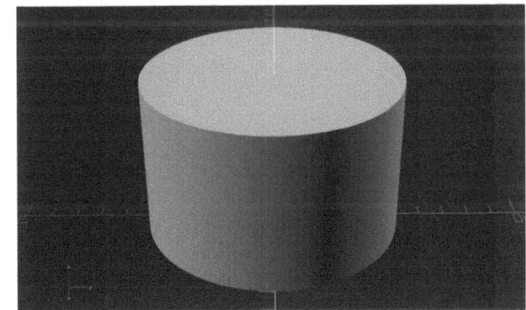

If the $fn value shloud only be changed for a certain primitive body, this is possible within the definition of the body:

```
cylinder(d=10, d2=0, h=6, $fn=4);
```

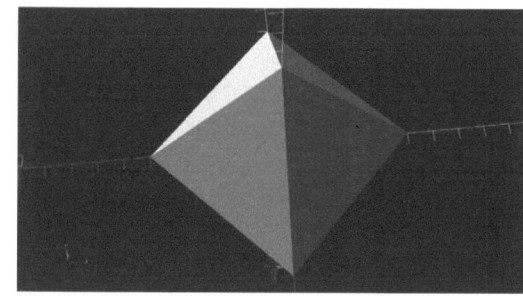

This can also be used to create some shapes that are not available in OpenSCAD. If the rounding of a cone is described with "only" 4 sides that result in a pyramid ...

A circle, described with "only" 3 faces, forms an equilateral triangle:

```
circle(12, $fn=3);
```

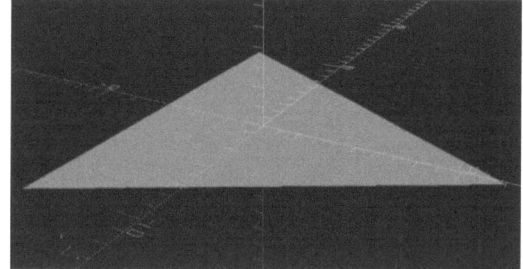

A hexagon or octagon could be const-ructed in the same way ...

Apart from $fn there are
- $fa ... minimum angles of faces and
- $fs ... minimum size of the faces available.

Here $fn takes precedence over all other values - so if you enter contradicting values for $fn and $fa or $fs, the other values are ignored and only $fn is considered!

$t - animation with OpenSCAD

The variable $t is not assigned directly, but multiplied by the parameter to be animated - for example:

```
$vpr = [35, 0, $t * 360];
linear_extrude(5)
  polygon([[0,0],[0,10],[14,0]]);
```

To start the animation, you have to show the animation bar with View -> Animation and then enter values for FPS (*frames per second*) and steps (*how many frames the animation consists of*):

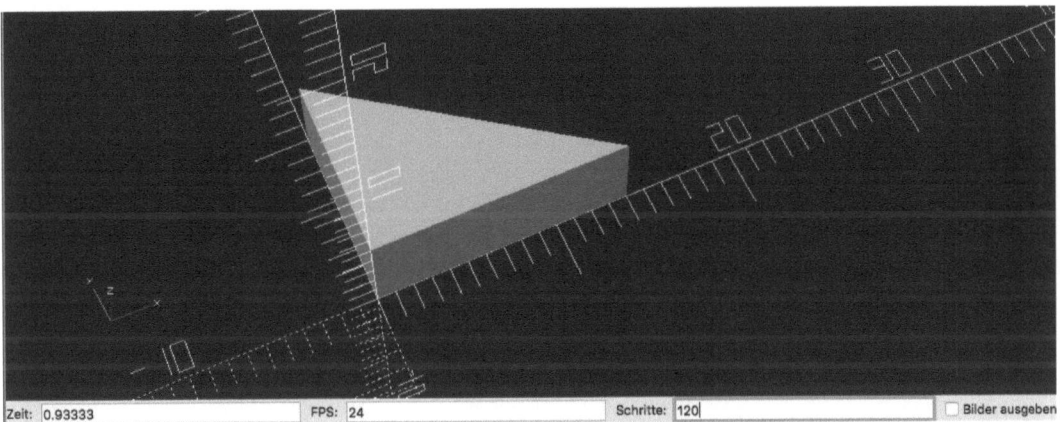

Here we got to know another group of special variables for view control:
- $vpr ... Camera angle in degrees for the X, Y and Z axes
- $vpd ... Camera distance - e.g. $vpd = 100;
- $vpt ... Camera offset to the left/right or up/down - e.g.:
  $vpt = [50, -10]; (*50 to the left and 10 to the top*)

SECTION 2

PRACTICAL EXAMPLES

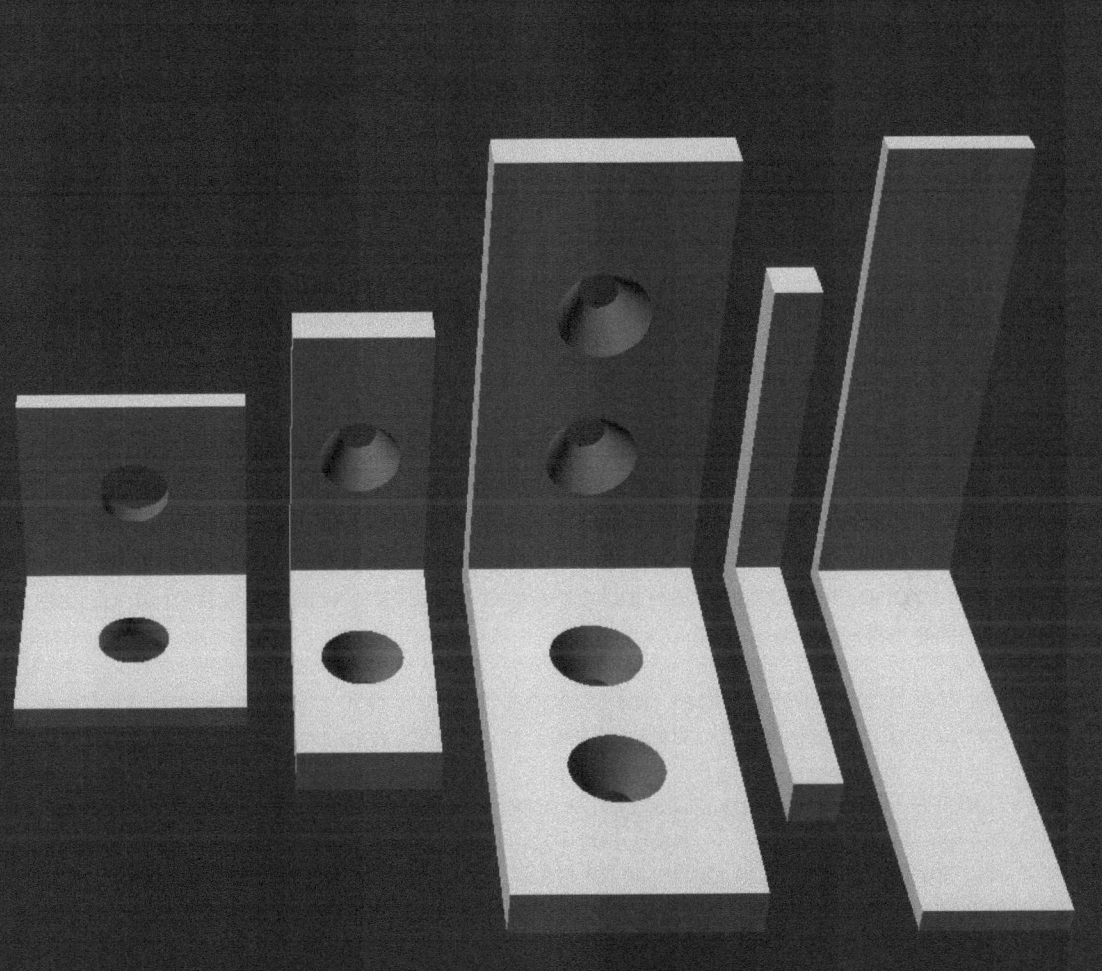

MODULES

Modules can be understood as a blueprint for a part. Let's look at the following code:

```
length = 12;
width = 8;
thickness = 2;

d1 = 2;
d2 = 5;

difference(){
    cube([length, width, thickness]);
    translate([length/2, width/2, -0.1])
      cylinder(d1=d1+0.1, d2=d2+0.1, h=thickness+0.2);
}
```

We use this to create a component with a central hole that is intended for a countersunk screw. If you would need several of these parts with different dimensions, you would have to copy the code over and over and adapt the variables. That would be difficult to maintain.

Whenever the basic design does not change or does not change much, but the same part could be needed in different sizes or variants, modules are ideal.

So let's turn the code into a module! Some readers may have noticed that I increase the diameters d1 and d2 by 0.1 each. I do this to compensate for the excess length of 0.2. If you are designing components for NASA, you will certainly have to work more carefully than simply adding 0.1 here and there. But for home 3D printing and even a lot of production parts that's enough!

```
$fn = 128;

module side(length, width, thickness, d1, d2){
    difference(){
        cube([length, width, thickness]);
        translate([length/2, width/2, -0.1])
            cylinder(d1=d1+0.1, d2=d2+0.1, h=thickness+0.2);
    }
}

side(length=12, width=8, thickness=2, d1=2, d2=5);
```

First, we create the module called side, and we create the variables as parameters that are transferred when the module is called.

So we can create our own commands like cube() or sphere()!

After defining the module, it must also be called. Without the call side(...); the module would not be drawn.

Can you already guess which part we are currently working on? Right, we will design an L - bracket for a screw connection. These parts are usually symmetrical, so we're going to create another module called bracket that uses the side module:

```
$fn = 128;

module bracket(length, width, thickness, d1, d2){
    module side(length, width, thickness, d1, d2){
        ...
    }
    translate([thickness, 0, 0]) rotate([0,-90,0])
```

```
    side(length=length, width=width, thickness=thickness, d1=d1,
        d2=d2);

    side(length=length, width=width, thickness=thickness, d1=d2,
        d2=d1);
}

bracket(length=12, width=8, thickness=2, d1=5, d2=2);
```

As you can see, modules can also be nested. The parameters are simply passed on by `bracket` to `side` ...

The construction of the bracket is very simple: We create one side, rotate it by -90° around the Y-axis and push it to the starting position with `translate()`.

In order not to have to mirror the lying side, I simply swapped the parameters `d1` and `d2` so that the hole points in the other direction.

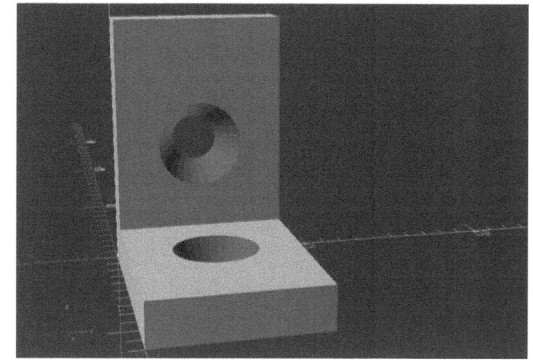

Here we notice that the holes are not quite centered. They are centered on each side of the bracket, but by overlapping the two sides to create the bracket, we should find the center of the free space. Therefore we adjust the following line in the module `side` again:

```
translate([[(length+thickness)/2, width/2, -0.1])
```

And the result looks now better.

What if we now had to create a model that also offers the option of up to two holes, as well as different holes for countersunk and flat head screws?

Then we need to give our model a little "intelligence":

```
module bracket(length, width,
thickness, d1, d2=0, offset1=0,
offset2=0){
```

First, we adapt the definition of the module - here with d2=0, so 0 is set as the standard value if d2 is not specified. Besides, we also define the values offset1 and offset2 with the standard value 0.

```
    module drill_hole(d1, d2){
        if(d2 == 0){
            cylinder(d=d1+0.1, h=thickness+0.2);
        }
        else{
            cylinder(d1=d1+0.1, d2=d2+0.1, h=thickness+0.2);
        }
    }
```

We create a separate sub-module for the hole and by checking whether d2 was specified or not with if(...) we accordingly create a cylinder for a straight hole with only one diameter or otherwise (else) a tapered cylinder with two diameters.

```
module side(length, width, thickness, d1, d2, offset1, offset2){
    difference(){
        cube([length, width, thickness]);
        if(offset1 == 0 && offset2 == 0){
            translate([(length+thickness)/2, width/2, -0.1])
                drill_hole(d1, d2);
        }

        if(offset1 != 0){
            translate([offset1, width/2, -0.1])
                drill_hole(d1, d2);
        }

        if(offset2 != 0){
            translate([offset2, width/2, -0.1])
                drill_hole(d1, d2);
        }
    }
}
```

We also add the parameters `offset1` and `offset2` to the module `side`. Here we no longer need to assign `0` as a standard value, since this has already happened with the `bracket` module!

Within the `difference` block, we check whether `offset1` and `offset2` have not been set and are therefore `0`. In this case, the hole is centered as usual. Besides, the `drill_hole` module is now called instead of the `cylinder` command.

If `offset1` or `offset2` were set to any value other than `0`, the code in the first `if` block would not be executed. Therefore, we do not need an `else` block at this point, but check directly with two further `if` queries whether `offset1` and `offset2` are not equal to `0`.

If this is the case, a hole is created and shifted by the value of `offset1` or `offset2`. That is why we create a `drill_hole` module. It is easier to maintain or improve instructions in a central place, for example in a module, instead of doing this spread over several places in the code.

```
    translate([thickness, 0, 0]) rotate([0,-90,0])
    side(length=length, width=width, thickness=thickness, d1=d1,
        d2=d2, offset1=offset1, offset2=offset2);

    translate([0, 0, thickness]) mirror([0,0,1])
    side(length=length, width=width, thickness=thickness, d1=d1,
        d2=d2, offset1=offset1, offset2=offset2);
}
```

A small adjustment also had to be made when creating the bracket from the two `side` elements. Since the `drill_hole` module now determines the type of hole with an `if` query, we cannot simply swap `d1` and `d2`. Instead, we now have to mirror the second side and then move it to the appropriate position.

The file is now ready. At this point, I also removed the call to `bracket(...)` and saved the file as `bracket_module.scad`!

That is the final version of `bracket_module.scad`:

```
$fn = 128;

module bracket(length, width, thickness, d1, d2=0, offset1=0, off-
set2=0){
    module drill_hole(d1, d2){
        if(d2 == 0){
            cylinder(d=d1+0.1, h=thickness+0.2);
        }
        else{
            cylinder(d1=d1+0.1, d2=d2+0.1, h=thickness+0.2);
        }
    }

    module side(length, width, thickness, d1, d2, offset1, offset2){
        difference(){
            cube([length, width, thickness]);
            if(offset1 == 0 && offset2 == 0){
                translate([(length+thickness)/2, width/2, -0.1])
                    drill_hole(d1, d2);
            }

            if(offset1 != 0){
                translate([offset1, width/2, -0.1])
                    drill_hole(d1, d2);
            }

            if(offset2 != 0){
                translate([offset2, width/2, -0.1])
                    drill_hole(d1, d2);
```

```
            }
        }
    }

// Assemble bracket
translate([thickness, 0, 0]) rotate([0,-90,0])
side(length=length, width=width, thickness=thickness, d1=d1,
     d2=d2, offset1=offset1, offset2=offset2);

translate([0, 0, thickness]) mirror([0,0,1])
side(length=length, width=width, thickness=thickness, d1=d1,
     d2=d2, offset1=offset1, offset2=offset2);
}
```

After that we create a file named `bracket_demo.scad` with the following content:

```
$fn = 128;
include <bracket_module.scad>;

bracket(length=12, width=8, thickness=2, d1=4, d2=2);

translate([0,10,0])
bracket(length=14, width=6, thickness=1, d1=2, offset1=11);

translate([0,18,0])
bracket(length=25, width=6, thickness=1, d1=2, offset1=9, off-
set2=17);

translate([0,26,0])
bracket(length=10, width=10, thickness=1, d1=3);

translate([0,38,0])
bracket(length=14, width=6, thickness=2, d1=3.5, d2=1.5);

translate([0,46,0])
bracket(length=22, width=10, thickness=2, d1=4, d2=1.5, offset1=8,
offset2=15);

translate([0,58,0])
bracket(length=16, width=2, thickness=2, d1=1, offset1=-8);

translate([0,62,0])
bracket(length=22, width=6, dicke=1, d1=1, offset1=-8);
```

After the rendering of the curves was fine-tuned with `$fn`, I used `include <bracket_module.scad>;` to make the code of the previously created file available in this file so that we can use is to create the following samples:

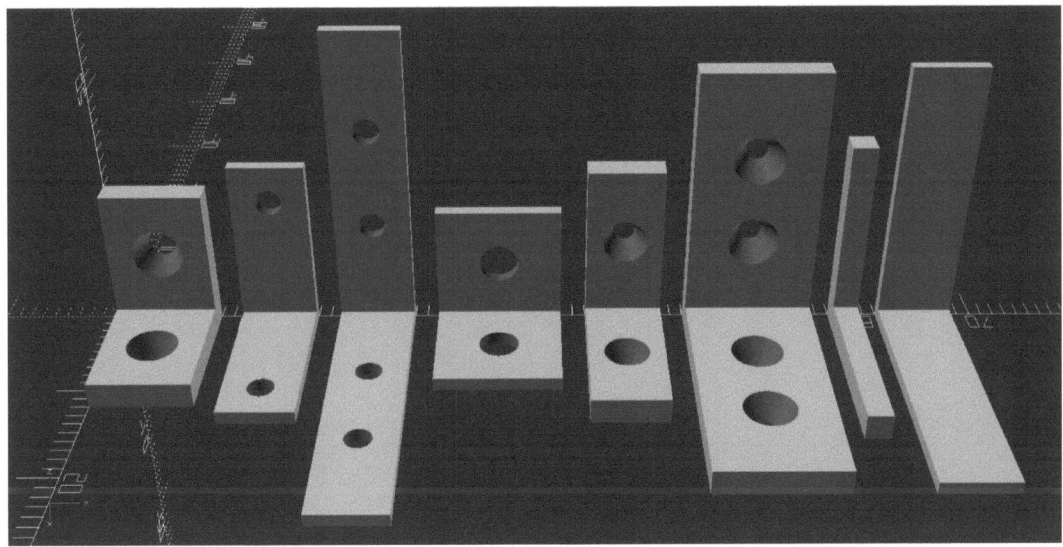

As you can see, the module can be used to create brackets in a wide variety of sizes with one, two or no holes. Besides, holes for countersunk and flat head screws can be made as required. Even placing a hole off-center is not a problem.

So you see the flexibility that can be incorporated into the models and how you can build your own library with components to implement larger projects.

LOOPS

In projects, it often happens that parts appear several times in the model. Whenever these multiple occurrences follow a logical pattern, such as a support every 10 units or a post every 20°, then loops are the method of choice:

```
$fn = 128;

r_outside = 40;
r_inside = 37;
height  = 1.6;

for(i=[0 : 30 : 330]){
    rotate([30, 0, i])
    difference(){
        cylinder(r=r_outside, h=height);
        translate([0, 0, -0.1])
          cylinder(r=r_inside, h=height+0.2);
    }
}

translate([0, 0, -20]) cylinder(r=r_outside-5.5, h=height);
```

The difference-command create a simple Ring with the parameters
r_outside, r_inside and height.

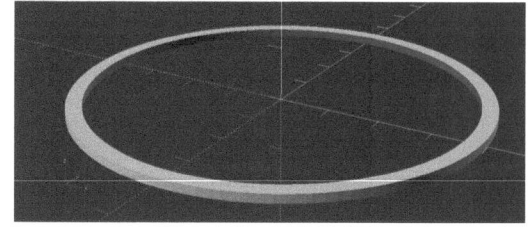

The `for`-loop creates hereby multiple rings. The parameters for the loop are [START : STEP : END].

The commands in the loop get also executed for i=0, i=30, i=60, ... i=330. If you alter the `for`-loop as follows
`for(i=[0 : 30 : $t*330]){`
you can use the animations function of Openscad to demonstrate what happens. You can open it with
`View -> Animation...`

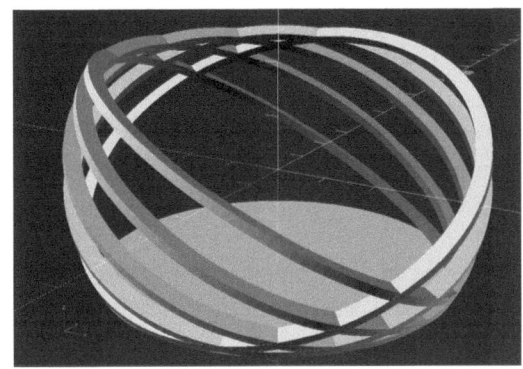

Then enter 2 in the FPS-field and 24 in the Steps-field. Now you should see how one ring after another gets added to the model.

The last line of the file creates the bottom for this model.

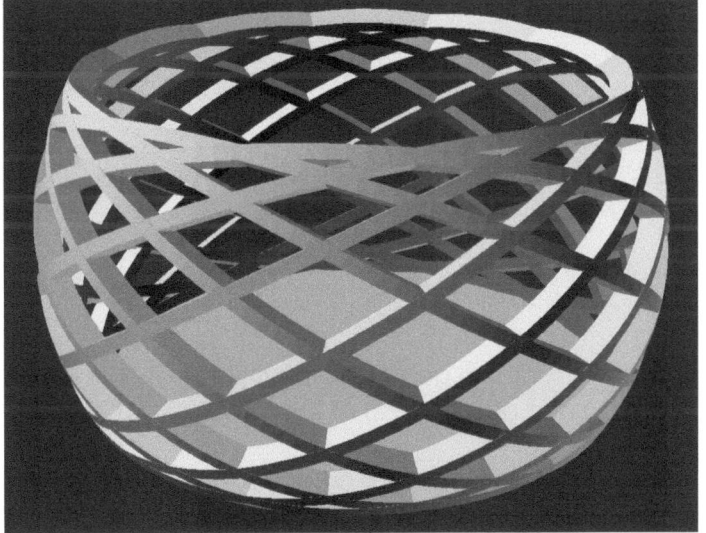

FUNCTIONS

What functions do in some programming languages is divided in OpenSCAD into modules for creating more complex forms and functions for calculating values and value lists.

For people with programming experience, it is at least a bit unusual but functions in OpenSCAD are basically just named formulas:

```
$fn = 128;
length = 60;
thickn = 4; // thickness
ds = 1;      // diam. for sphere

function rhomb(l=1, w=1, offs=0)
  = [
      [0,0],
      [w,0],
      [offs+w, l],
      [offs, l]
    ];
```

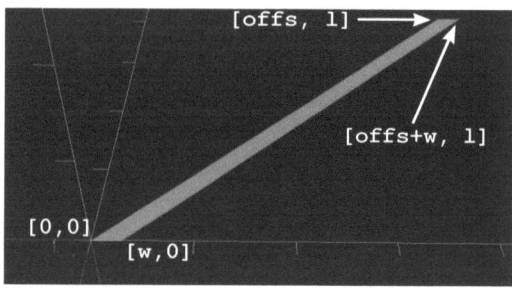

```
function pyth(c)
  = sqrt(pow(c,2) / 2);
```

The `rhomb` function generates the coordinates of a rhombus based on the length (`l`), width (`w`) and offset (`offs`) of the top side. (see sketch)

The `pyth` function provides a transformation of the Pythagorean Theorem to calculate the length of `l` and `offs` for the desired length of the slope.

If we look at the call to rhomb(l = pyth(length) - ds, w = thickn-1, offs = pyth(length) - ds), we see that l and offs should be of the same so that we create an angle of 45°.

Therefore we can reshape the Pythagorean theorem as $c^2 = a^2 + a^2$ or $c^2 = a^2 \times 2$. That leads to the reshape a = squareroot (sqrt) of c^2 (pow(c,2)) : 2!

If we would have made an error in this formula, then it would be better to be able to fix this error at a central point instead of spreading it out in the code. Functions are ideal for such situations. Besides, libraries with frequently required items such as the coordinates of a trapezoid, a rhombus, etc. can be built with functions.

```
difference() {
  // Used to get round corners
  minkowski() {
    rotate([90, 45, 90])
    linear_extrude(thickn*2-ds) {
      // long side
      polygon(
        rhomb(l=pyth(length)-ds,
          w=thickn-1,
          offs=pyth(length)-ds));

      // short side
      rotate([0, 0, 45])
      polygon(
        rhomb(l=pyth(length)/3,
          w=thickn-1,
          offs=pyth(length)/3));
    }
```

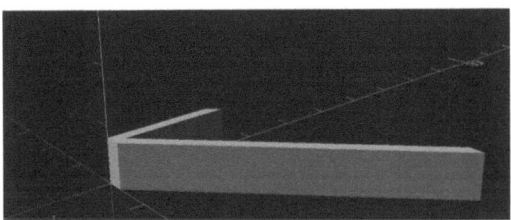

Fig.: linear_extrude(thickn*2-ds)

Fig.: rotate((90, 45, 90)) ... X-axis (90°)

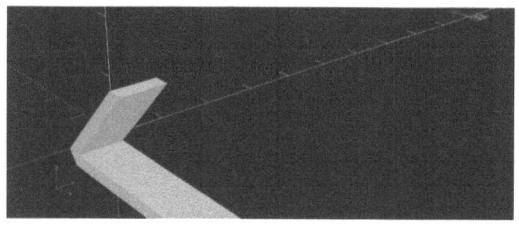

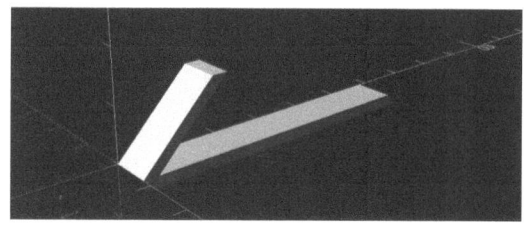

Fig.: rotate((90, 45, 90)) ... Y-axis (45°)   *Fig.: rotate((90, 45, 90)) ... Z-axis (90°)*

```
    // to create the round corners
    sphere(d=ds);
}

// Debug-output in OpenSCAD console
echo ("Ramboid length:", pyth(length));

// drill holes
translate([thickn - ds/2, length-12, -thickn])
cylinder(d=2, h=thickn+ds);

translate([thickn - ds/2, length-24, -thickn])
cylinder(d=2, h=thickn+ds);
}
```

The `minkowski` command in connection with a sphere extends a 3D object on all edges by the radius of the sphere - therefore the diameter of the sphere (`ds`) was subtracted from the `width`, thickness (`thickn`) and height (`linear_extrude`). If you don't do that the `minkowski` command grows this 3D model forwards, backwards, downwards, upwards, left and right by the radius of the sphere.

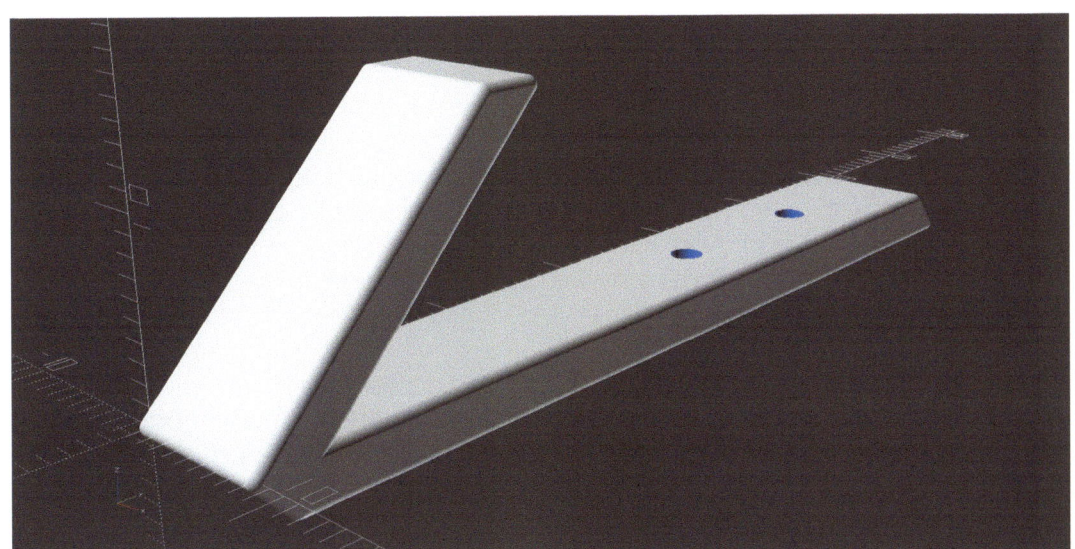

We can also see in the two pictures how the `minkowski` command stretches in all directions.

Since now 0.5 units of the thickness grow in the positive and 3.5 units in the negative Z-direction, the `translate` command was selected for the hole as shown on the left side.

Since the extrusion is 2 x `thickn` we have to use after the `minkowski` command, an offset of the hole corresponds to `thickn - ds/2` in the X direction to get the center. With `length - 12` and `24`, we set an offset of the hole from above. Finally, the Z offset of `-thickn` (*-4*) ensures that a cylinder with the length of 5 (`h = thickn+ds`) pierces an object completely, which is in Z-direction from -3.5 up to +0.5.

As you can see, the use of the `minkowski` command often means that you have to be a little more careful in your models, as the offset of parts or their position in space change slightly.

If your height specification for the cylinder were, for example, `h = thickn + 1`, then this would work with `ds = 1`, but as soon as `ds` were greater than 2, the hole could no longer penetrate the part! And with `ds = 2` you run into danger that there are some artifacts in the final model. That's why we used in our model `h = thickn + ds` to compensate for possible changes in `ds`.

Just try the change and play through all of these cases! The reason why I am talking about that in such detail at this point is that I find an error in many models - mixing up of parameters and fixed numerical values. Basically, this is not a problem. In this model, I have used that too and written that the length of the short side should be approximately 33% of the long side (`l = pyth(length) / 3`).

At this point, the number 3 cannot cause any problems. The offset of the holes from above (`length-12` or `length-24`) can in the worst case cause a hole beeing covered by the short side (*e.g. with* `length = 35` *and below*).

If, however, fixed numerical values occur for the positioning or lengths of cutouts, drill holes, etc. together with the minkowski command, a change in the corner radius may result in parts not fitting perfectly together or dimensions of cutouts, etc. not fitting.

Now you know who is the "main suspect" in such a case! The modifiers !, # and * are particularly useful for checking what exactly happens. Apart from that, as in this example, you can use `echo("Ramboid length", pyth(length));` to output values or calculation results in the console, which creates a line like this:

```
ECHO: "Ramboid length", 42.4264
```

```
Compiling design (CSG Tree generation)...
ECHO: "Ramboid length:", 42.4264
Compiling design (CSG Products generation)...
Geometries in cache: 123
Geometry cache size in bytes: 6615312
CGAL Polyhedrons in cache: 26
CGAL cache size in bytes: 89945608
Compiling design (CSG Products normalization)...
Normalized CSG tree has 3 elements
Compile and preview finished.
Total rendering time: 0 hours, 0 minutes, 0 seconds
```

TEXT

In this example, we want to work a little with the `text` command and create a stamp. This is rather difficult to do with a filament printer, but resin printers, which have been getting cheaper and cheaper lately, in combination with a flexible resin, can easily produce such stamp plates in suitable quality.

```
cube([70, 45, 2]);

mirror([1,0,0])
translate ([-70,0,0])
linear_extrude(height=3.25){
    translate([1.2, 38])
      text("MAXIMILIAN CADMÜLLER", size=4.5, spacing=0.9);
    translate([1.2, 31]) text("OpenSCAD Entwickler", size=4.5);
    translate([1.2, 23]) text("Designstraße 13a", size=4.5);
    translate([1.2, 17]) text("A-1010 Wien", size=4.5);
    translate([1.2, 10]) text("+43 1 123 456", size=3.5);
    translate([1.2, 3])  text("AT U1234567890", size=3.5);
}
```

The innermost block is basically just texts that are brought to the appropriate position with `translate`. In the `text` command, you set the direction (*left to right or right to left*) with `direction = "ltr"` or `rtl`. In addition, the vertical and horizontal alignment of the text can be controlled with `valign =` or `halign =` (*see documentation*). With `size =` you set the

font size in units as you surely guessed and the `spacing = 0.9` of the first line shortens the spacing between the letters of that line...

Then `translate([-70,0,0])` moves the entire text into the negative area of the X-axis and `mirror([1,0,0])` mirrors the texts along the X-axis back to the original position.

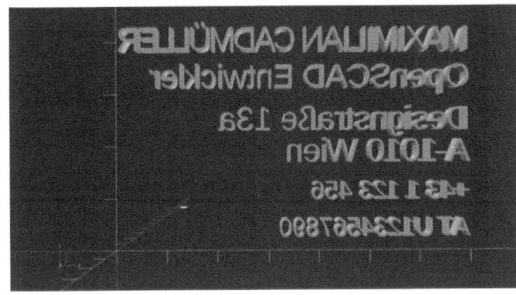

It is important to note that the mirroring does not take place over the axis but along the axis! In addition, the original is changed and no copy is made. So if you need to compose an object from two symmetrical halves, then you either have to make a module out of the half and then use `half();` and `mirror([1,0,0]) half();` or you can use a loop:

```
for(i=[0:1:1]){
    mirror([i,0,0]) ...
```

The first line with `cube(...);` create a base plate on which the letters were finally placed. This helped with the placement of the lines and to pick the right font size.

The height of the text is slightly more than one unit taller than the plate. So that fits perfectly for the print - in the end, the letters should have risen between 1 and 1.5mm for a stamp.

Now that we can manufacture a stamping plate, we want to quickly create a stamp body as well...

```
$fn=128;

difference(){
    hull(){
        cube([72, 47, 4],
            center=true);
        cylinder(d=10, h=45);
    }

    translate([-46,25,41])
      rotate([90, 0, 0])
        cylinder(d=80, h=50);
    translate([46,25,41])
      rotate([90, 0, 0])
        cylinder(d=80, h=50);
}

translate([0,0,55]) sphere(20);
```

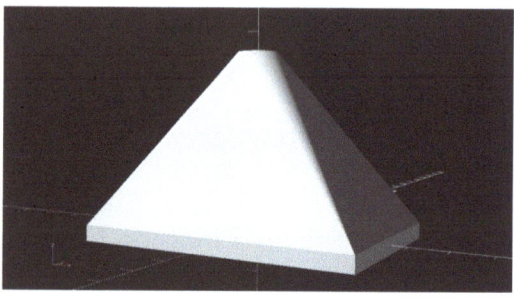

Fig.: hull() of cube(...) and cylinder(...)

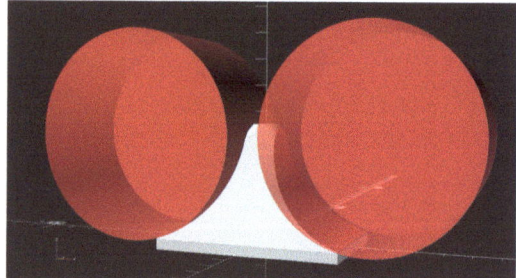

Fig: difference() of hull() and 2 x cylinder(...)

I made a conscious decision to make the base of the body 2mm larger in the X and Y directions to make it easier to attach the stamp plate.

With `hull()` we create a pointed body, from which we subtract two large cylinders with `difference()`. We did that to get a more traditional shape and to save material and printing time as well.

Last but not least, a ball with a diameter of 40 units is placed on our stamp and the model is ready.

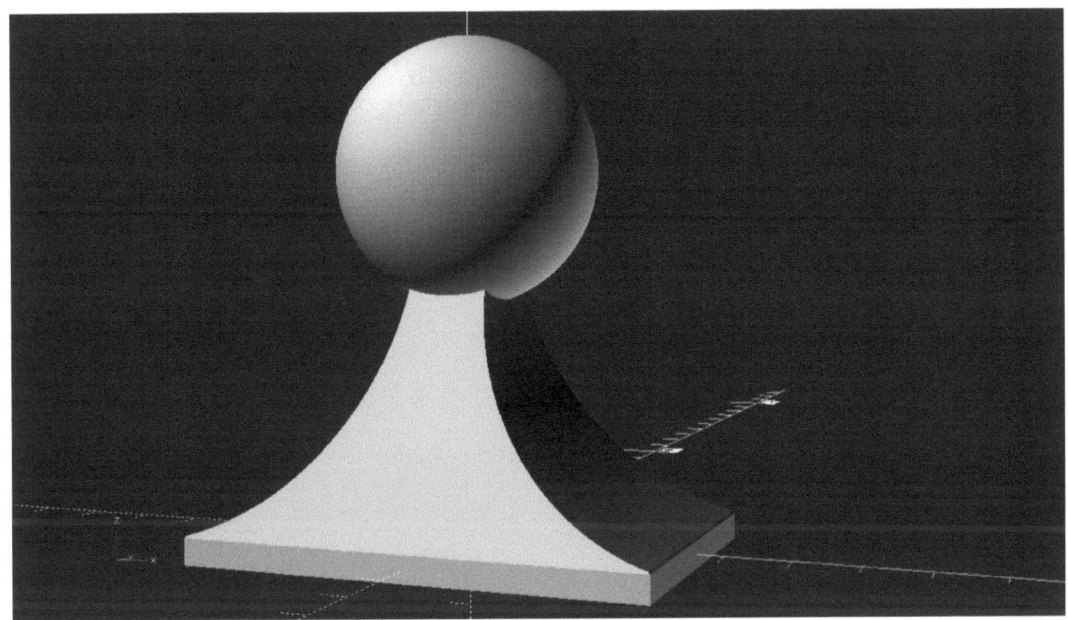

As cylinders and spheres get created in a centered position I used rather the parameter `center=true` in the `cube()` then moving the cylinder within the `hull()` and the `sphere()`. If possible I prefer to work with just one axis in `translate()` to make the code easier readable.

I only needed two sizes at this point so I used no parameters. As an exercise, however, you are welcome to add parameters to the model so that you can vary the size more easily.

MULTMATRIX

Next, we want to demystify the "nightmare" of many OpenSCAD users a little... After this lesson, you will really understand the `multmatrix` command and be able to use it correctly...

```
// Cardholder
difference(){
    multmatrix([
    [1, 0, 0, 0],
    [0, 1, 0.4, 0],
    [0, 0, 1, 0],
    [0, 0, 0, 1]
    ])
        difference(){
            cube([100, 30, 48]);
            translate([3,3,3])
                cube([94, 24, 48]);
        }
```

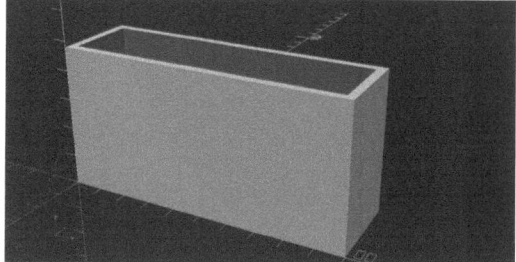

Fig. difference() of 2 cube(...)-objects

First, we create a cuboid and then another cuboid that is 6 units smaller in the X and Y directions, which we subtract from the first one.

With the offset of 3 units in each direction, we end up with an open cuboid as shown in the first picture.

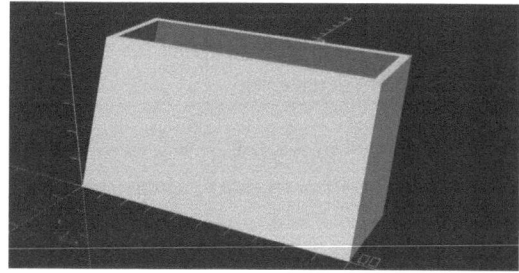

Fig. multmatrix()

Then the open rectangle is tilted backward by 19.2 units (*factor* 0.4). We will explain why this is so following the example...

```
translate([25, 28, 44])
  rotate([180, 0, 0]) hull(){
    cube([50, 10, 0.1]);
    translate([-5, -5, -5])
      cube([60, 20, 0.1]);
}

translate([49, -10, 4])
  cube([2, 35, 37]);
for(i=[4 : 4 : 44]){
    translate([49-i, -10,
               4+i/4*1.5])
      cube([2, 35, 37-i/4*3]);
    translate([49+i, -10,
               4+i/4*1.5])
      cube([2, 35, 37-i/4*3]);
}
}
```

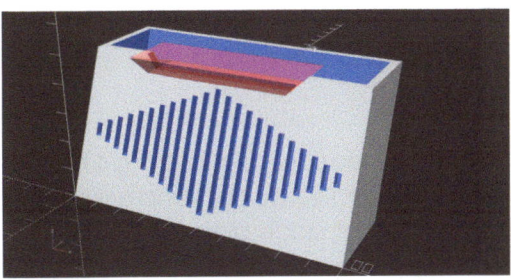
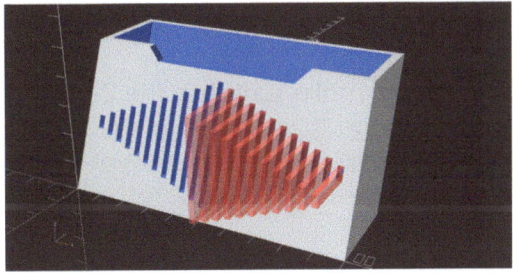

An upside-down trapezoid and other narrow cuboids are then subtracted from this body. We construct the trapezoid using `hull()` over two `cube()`-objects. One was made 10 units smaller in the X and 5 units smaller in the Y direction and then offset by half the size difference in the X and Y directions. The Z offset of 5 units then gives the trapezoid its height.

Since you cannot join `square()`-objects (*2D*) in 3D space with the `hull` command to form a body, I used a `cube()` with a height of 0.1 units instead. You can get closer to a perfect surface with e.g. 0.01 units or even smaller values for the height. I try not to

75

be overly precise in such workarounds. It just makes no difference at all to 3D printing and most other manufacturing processes!

Then I construct a narrow cuboid that is 2 units wide and is indented 49 units in the X-direction. This means that the center of the rectangle is 50 units and so exactly at the center of the cardholder.

With a `for` loop, we count from 4 in steps of 4 to 44 ($i = [4:4:44]$) and create two rectangles for each pass, at an offset of which is either $49-i$ or $49+i$. So that new cuboids get created from the center onward in both directions of the X-axis.

You should make sure that the Z-offset is large enough to cut through the sloping surface at all points, but not yet pierce the rear wall!

```
// Base
hull(){
    cube([100, 30, 0.1]);
    translate([-5, -5, -5])
      cube([110, 40, 0.1]);
}
```

Finally, a trapezoid was put together from two cuboids using `hull()` to create a base. In order not to move the whole object, I constructed the base in the negative Z-direction.

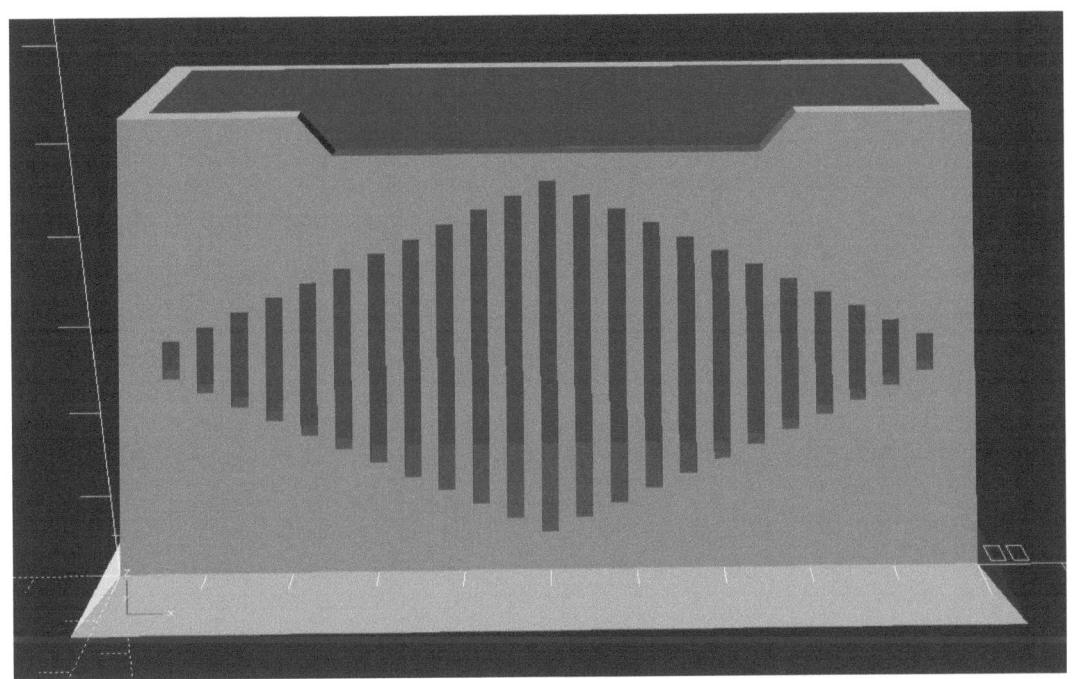

When exporting to an STL file, it makes no difference and all parts, regardless of whether they are in a positive or negative direction, are exported.

Such an STL file then contains a body which can then be placed anywhere in the slicer or another CAD program.

Here, too, I did the model without parameters, since business cards have a certain format and I saw no point in designing the model in such a way that it can be changed in size quickly and easily - but you are welcome to do that as an exercise!

MULTMATRIX IN DETAIL

When using the `multmatrix()` command, either the body or the matrix should be "normalized" (*consisting exclusively of values between 0 and 1*). In simple terms, we can say that the offset works like the scaling - for each unit in the corresponding direction of the original body, the units specified in the offset are shifted. Therefore, two identical bodies can be created in the following two ways:

```
multmatrix([
    [1, 0, 0.5, 0],
    [0, 1, 0.4, 0],
    [0, 0, 1, 0],
    [0, 0, 0, 1]
    ])
    cube([100, 30, 48]);

color("yellow")
translate([120,0,0])
multmatrix([
    [100, 0, 24, 0],
    [0, 30, 19.2, 0],
    [0, 0, 48, 0],
    [0, 0, 0, 1]
    ]) cube([1, 1, 1]);

#translate([48*0.5, 48*0.4, 48])
cube([220, 1, 1]);
```

The size of this `cube()` is specified as [100, 30, 48], and the cuboid, therefore, has a height of 48. The shear of the Z-axis in the X direction is 0.5 and in the Y direction 0.4 units per unit in the Z direction of the original cuboid.

The second `cube()` only measures [1, 1, 1] units and is scaled to [100, 30, 48] with the matrix, here 24 is the shear of the Z-axis in the X direction and 19.2 is the shear in the Y direction.

Last but not least, a cuboid is used as a yardstick. The dimensions are 220 units (*100 + 20 distance + 100*) in the X direction and 1 each in the Y and Z directions. With translate we bring it to position 24 (*48 * 0.5*) in the X direction and 19.2 (*48 * 0.4*) in the Y direction and as you can see it sits perfectly on all edges and is absolutely flush!

This makes the calculation method of this command actually obvious:

The 0.5 or 0.4 units of shear for each of the 48 height units correspond exactly to the 24 or 19.2 units of shear for the second cuboid with the height of 1.

Practically I don't use the offsets in `multmatrix` and combine it as needed with a `translate` command to indicate more clearly what is going on in the model. The same is valid for scaling models. In my opinion, using the `multmatrix` "just" for shearing makes models more self-explanatory!

TWIST

The `twist` parameter of `linear_extrude()` makes it possible to rotate a 2D shape around its center axis when extruding to create interesting shapes.

```
$fn = 128;

module base(l=100, r=10){
    minkowski(){
        square(l-r*2, center=true);
        circle(r=r);
    }
}

wall = 2;
height  = 135;

linear_extrude(height, twist=height)
  difference(){
    base();
    offset(-wall) base();
}

translate([0,0,-wall*1.5])
linear_extrude(wall*1.5)
  base();
```

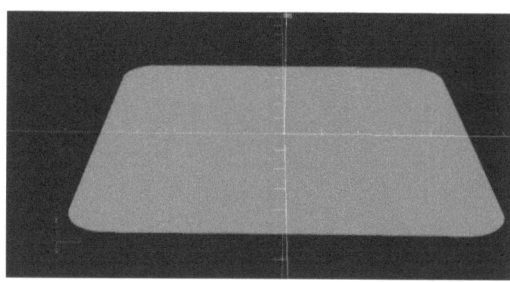

Abb. base()

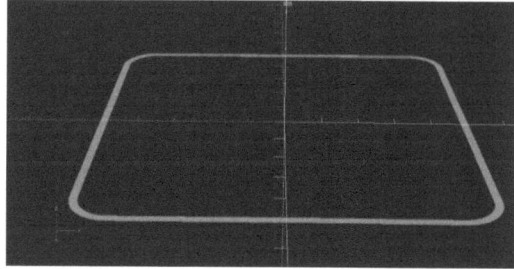

Abb. difference() without linear_extrude(...)

The module `base()` with the `minkowski()` of the two 2D elements should be clear ...

The reason why we are working with 2D objects at this point is that `linear_extrude()` only works with 2D objects, just like `offset()`.

With `difference()` we create a 2D exterior wall with a thickness according to the `wall` parameter, which we then extrude by 135 units with `linear_extrude` and rotate by 1° for each unit with `twist=height`.

Finally, another `base` is placed, extruded and shifted down by its height to form the bottom of this vase.

If you wish to twist the bottom as well you can reach that with:

```
mirror([0,0,1])
   linear_extrude(wall*1.5,
      twist=-wall*1.5) base();
```

... instead of the `translate` and `linear_extrude` commands shown before.

WORKING WITH DXF-FILES

Often you get construction drawings from other CAD programs with which you want to work.

As a small example, I created the following drawing in LibreCAD:

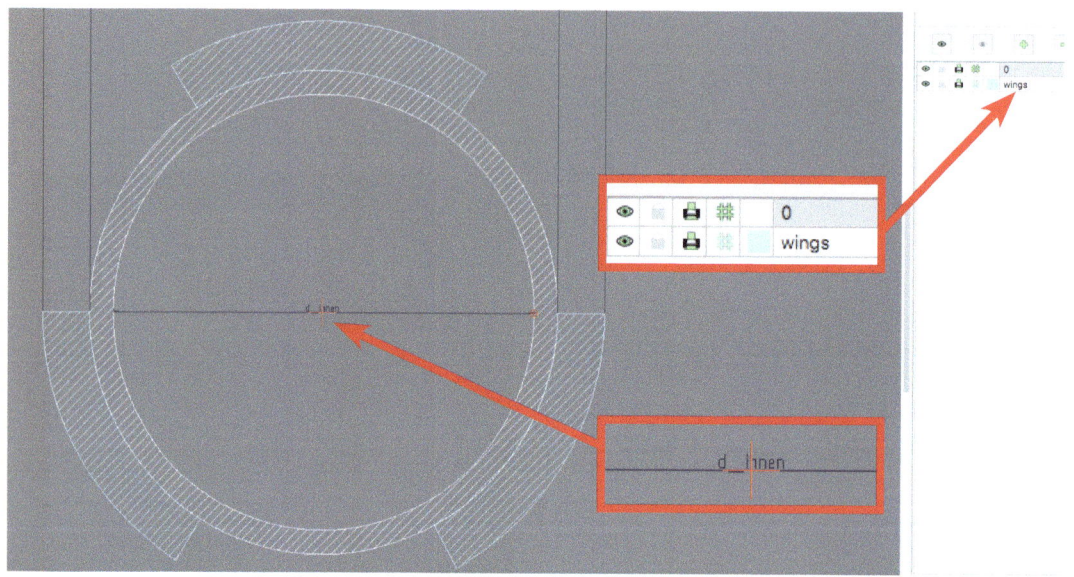

Hereby the pipe was constructed on Layer 0 and the wings on the layer wings. The reason to separate them we will see soon.

I have also given the dimensioning for the inner diameter of the pipe the name d_innen, to be able to access this value later.

```
$fn = 128;

h_pipe  = 90;
h_wing  = 6;
d_inner = dxf_dim(file="Connector.dxf", name="d_innen", layer="0");

difference(){
    linear_extrude(h_pipe)
    import(file="Connector.dxf",
            layer="0");

    #translate([0,0,h_pipe-3.1])
    cylinder(d1=d_inner-0.1,
            d2=d_inner+6, h=3.2);
}

linear_extrude(h_wing)
import(file="Connector.dxf", layer="wings");
```

First I set the render quality and create two parameters for the extrusion height of the pipe (h_pipe) and the wings (h_wing).

With dxf_dim(...) I pull the value of the linear dimension with the name d_innen from layer 0. You could not specifiy the layer parameter, but since we want to be on the safe side and don't want to accidentally read out the wrong dimensions from another layer. So I always specify the layer parameter, especially when I work with files from others!

Within the difference() block we import the content of level 0 without the dimensioning as a 2D object and then convert this into a 3D object with linear_extrude().

From the resulting object, we then subtract a 3.2 unit high cone, which causes a 3.1 unit long and 3 unit wide bevel on the inner edge of the pipe.

Just imagine that the component was a connection piece and another pipe would have to be inserted at this point...

Then the 2D shape of the wings layer is simply loaded and extruded.

In this example, you can also see how a DXF file must be structured so that you can easily use individual parts and measured values.

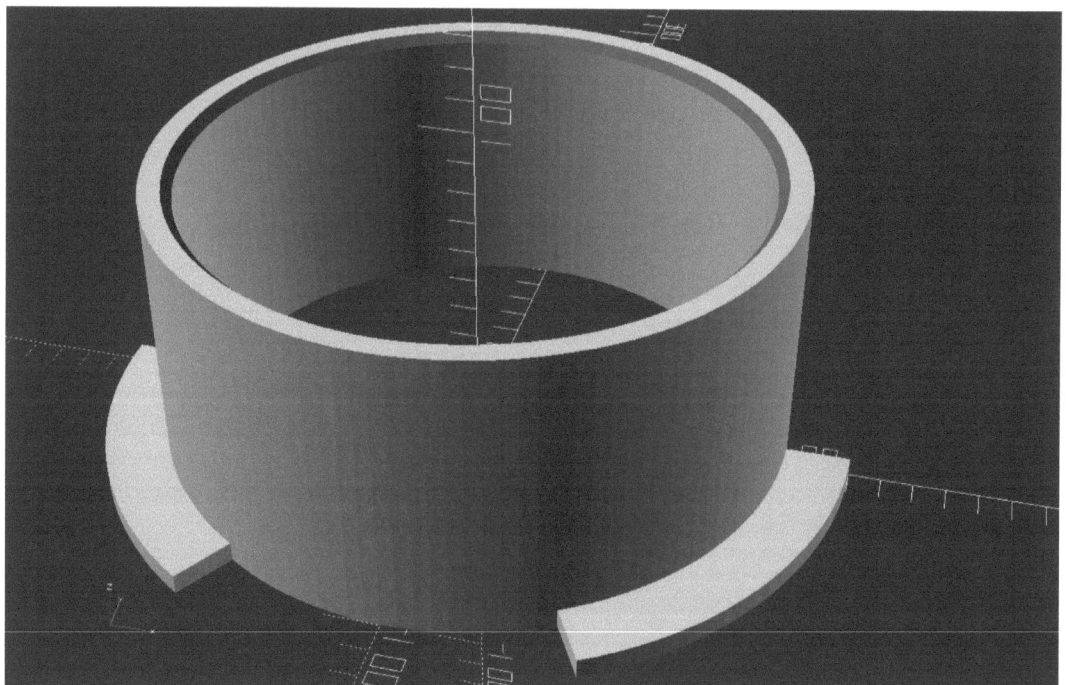

Of course, you can handle the imported shapes as every other self-created object. So you could write

```
!rotate_extrude()
  translate([100,100,0])
    difference(){
      import(file="pipe.dxf",
        layer="0");
      square(120);
}
```

to create a candle holder with an integrated bowl for decorative stones.

Or:

```
!rotate_extrude()
  resize([150, 220])
    translate([100,100,0])
      difference(){
        import(file="pipe.dxf",
                layer="0");
        translate([-50,0,0])
          square(150);
}
```

WORKING WITH STL-FILES

In case you wish to import 3D shapes you could use STL-files:

```
import(file="spool_holder.stl");
#translate([-117, 32, 0]) cube([6.8, 6.8, 25]);
```

For this, I imported the spool-holder for an Anycubic i3 Mega from the user `Domi1988`
(`https://www.thingiverse.com/thing:2670776`).

I like this spool holder. However, as you can see here, the hole for the screw is so close to the edge that the spool holder tends to break after a short period.

When importing, an object may be placed at any position in space. You can see that very well in the picture below. Instead of lying with any edge in the zero points, the component floats somewhere in 3D space.

This also results in the coordinates for the `translate` command!

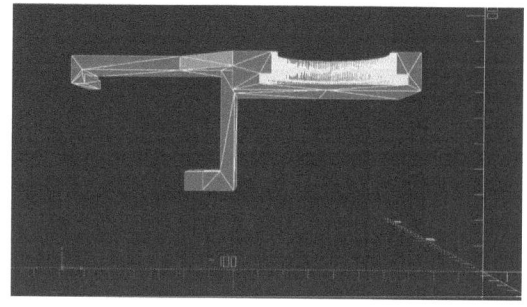

Instead of using the trial and error method to bring the component to a logical zero point and then measuring the printed component with the vernier caliper, I created my "extension" by estimating the position and dimensions of the cube() and constantly updating the preview. Since the guessing game about positioning the original component at a zero point would be necessary anyway, I can also play it with the cube() and save myself having to measure.

Of course, such an imported component can be treated like any other 3D object. However, it is a single part and you can no longer access the individual primitive parts that make up the object!

CHECK ACCURACY OF FIT

You may check with

```
difference(){
  import(file="spool_holder.stl");
  translate([-117, 32, 0])
    cube([6.8, 6, 24]);
}
```

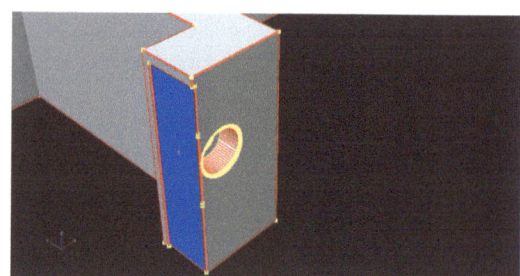

if the added part fits exactly.

For this demonstration, I altered the size of the `cube()` a bit.

Here for the menu option `View -> Show Edges` comes in handy because so you can see thin indents and leftovers much better.

Another option would be to place a huge `cube()` roughly and use `intersection()` to create a fitting part, which can be re-sized with `scale()`.

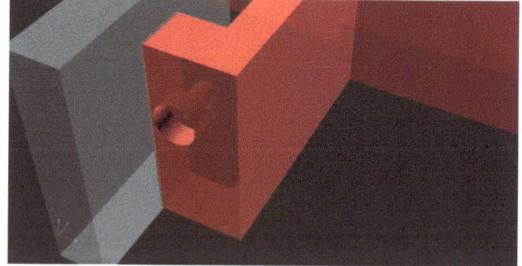

In that case, the scale command moves the `intersection`-part around because it also scales the offset from the center-point and that results in this code:

```
import(file="spool_holder.stl");

translate([2093.5, 0, 0])
scale([20, 1, 1])
intersection(){
        import(file="spool_holder.stl");
        translate([-120.2, 20, -3]) cube([10, 40, 30]);
}
```

Which way you choose, is up to you. In my opinion, the intersection-method is less clear and needs more tries to dial it in!

SECTION 3

WORKFLOW FROM THE IDEA

TO THE FINNISHED 3D PRINT

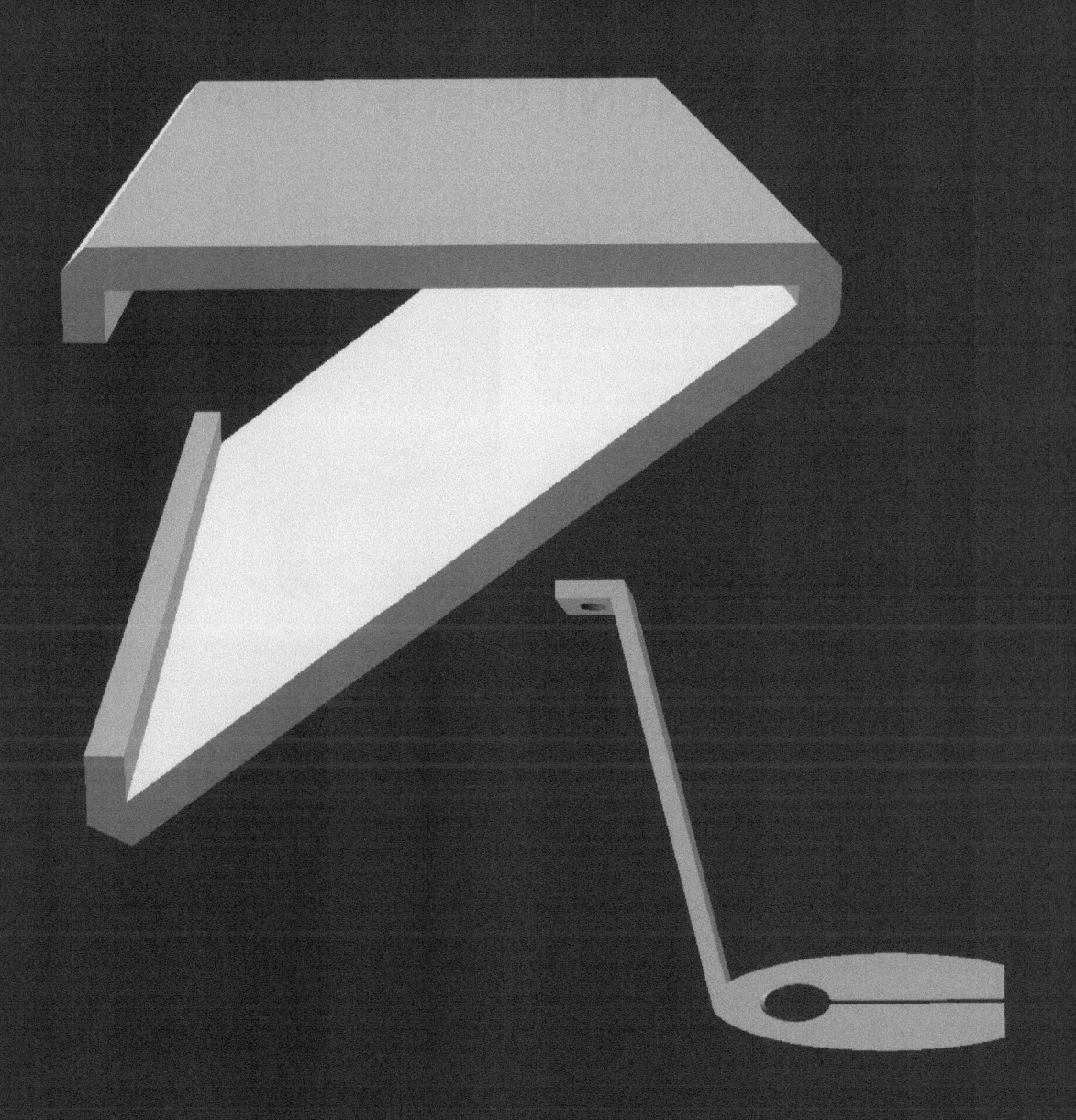

A COMPONENT GETS CREATED

PREPARATION & DESIGN-CONCEPT

The specific problem we want to solve is to keep the hotend cables and the filament guide tube of my Anycubic i3 Mega, from becoming wedged under the upper L-rail of the Z-axis frame.

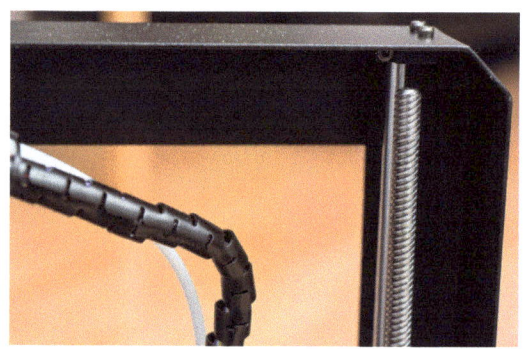

Before we get started and create a design, we must first think about how the part should look and how the required function could be implemented.

My first idea was a clamp that was supposed to fix an old ski pass holder to the Z-frame, which keeps the cables on tension and at the same time guides them.

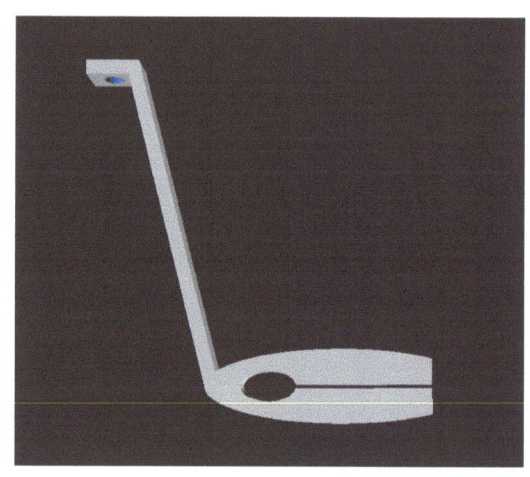

The corresponding part could look like this or something similar. But I immediately dropped this idea because I rarely make such high prints and therefore the cable or the connections would be permanently under tension, which in long-term use would certainly not be very good for the durability of the printer.

Besides, I don't know whether the pull mechanism of the ski pass holder can withstand this load in long-term use either.

So I needed to have a different idea. When the open edge of the profile gets closed with a straight line, a slope is created that would lead the cables to the outside with minimal stress. Even if the pulling force of the ski pass holder wouldn't be very high, but after the printer is constantly moving, the following applies: "Constant dripping wears away the stone!"

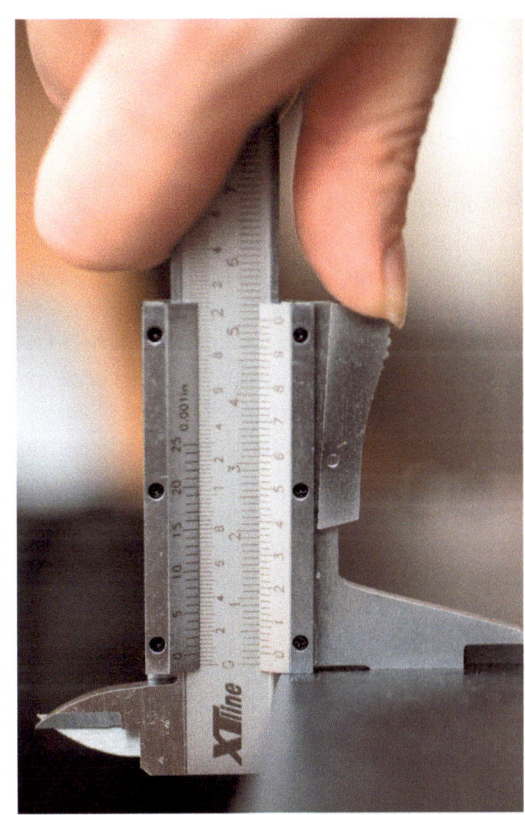

So it's time to measure - here I determined a material thickness of 1.4mm with the caliper.

Furthermore, the length of the upper edge was 51.6mm and the height of the front 40.4mm.

I rounded these values to 52 or 41mm for the model. The 3D printer itself has a tolerance of +/- 0.1mm if it is well configured and therefore the parts should fit very well and tightly with the dimensions specified by me.

DESIGN IN OPENSCAD

First I put the values in variables at this point. In my opinion, this increases the legibility of the code, and I also expect one or the other millimeter of series fluctuations with such Chinese products.

I intended 3.2mm as the thickness of the clamp (`wall`), as this is a multiple of 0.4mm which is the nozzle diameter on my printer.

Since the inner shape can be constructed quite easily with 4 points, I have chosen a polygon at this point. That makes it also possible to use the offset command to create an identical shape with outer edges in the distance of the variable `wall`.

This time I didn't make a module out of the polygon, but just stored the coordinates in a variable called `points`. This serves the same purpose in this case and therefore I wanted to introduce this variant to you as well.

After the inner shape was expanded by 3.2 units, I removed the original inner shape and a rectangle from it to create a clamp-shape. The rectangle was dimensioned so that it is 6 units shorter than the `L_height` and placed in such a way that 3 units of overhang remain as retaining clips at the top and bottom.

The required length of the rail would be 335mm - I decided at this point for extrusion of 100 units, as this does not make the material too stiff. Apart from that, my i3 only has a build-height of 210mm ...

The remaining not quite 2cm per side allow you to get behind the panels with a finger and remove them more easily. Since the cable runs up in a curve anyway, the omitted corners do not interfere with the function.

```
L_width = 52;
L_height  = 41;
L_thickness  = 1.4;
wall = 3.2;

points = [
    [0, 0],
    [L_width, 0],
    [L_width, -L_height],
    [0, -L_thickness]
];

linear_extrude(100)
difference(){
    offset(delta=wall,
           chamfer=true)
      polygon(points);

    polygon(points);

    translate([L_width-3,
               -L_height+4])
      square([10, L_height-6]);
}
```

Fig. polygon(points)

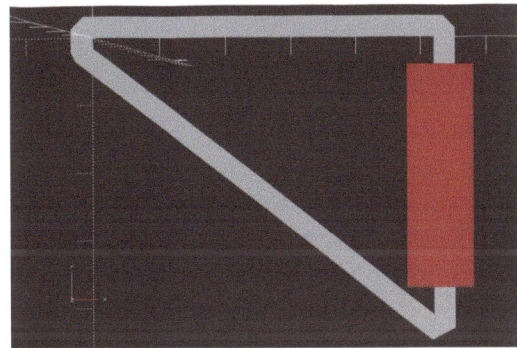

Fig. difference()

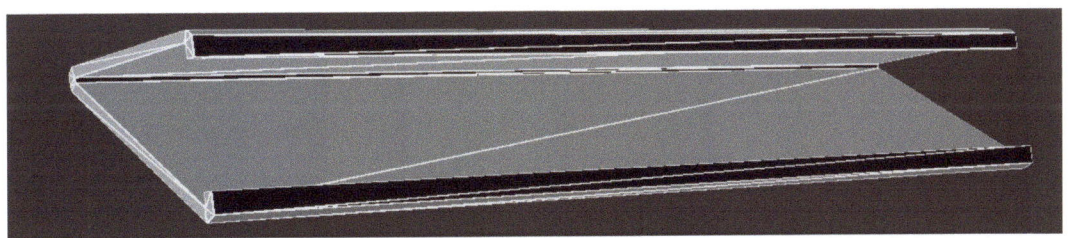

STL-EXPORT

You can export an STL-file by the following two methods:
1) `File` -> `Export` -> `STL export...`
2) By clicking the STL-button in the toolbar of the editor (*see screenshot*)

Hereby the result of the last rendering pass is exported. If you have made changes and have not re-rendered, you will be asked whether you want to export the last rendered version.

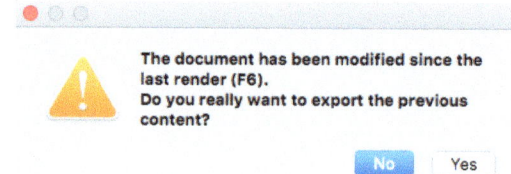

With `no`, you cancel the export. You have to trigger the rendering yourself either with the `F6` key or via the menu `Design` -> `Render`, or via the render button to the left of the STL button in the editor window.

When exporting, a simple save dialog is displayed with which you can specify where the exported file gets saved. (*This process is of course the same for all other export formats*)

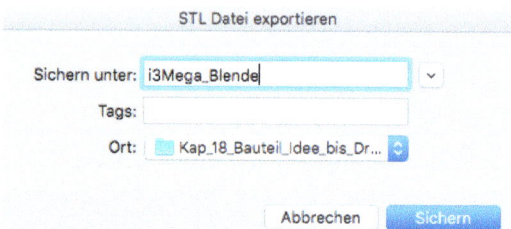

SLICING FOR 3D-PRINTING

When slicing, I deliberately printed the brackets upright and not lying down. So I save myself creating a support structure and cleaning the print afterward, but what is much more important is, that the load when pulling the clamps apart to apply them is rotated by 90° to the layer structure. That makes the clamp much more stable!

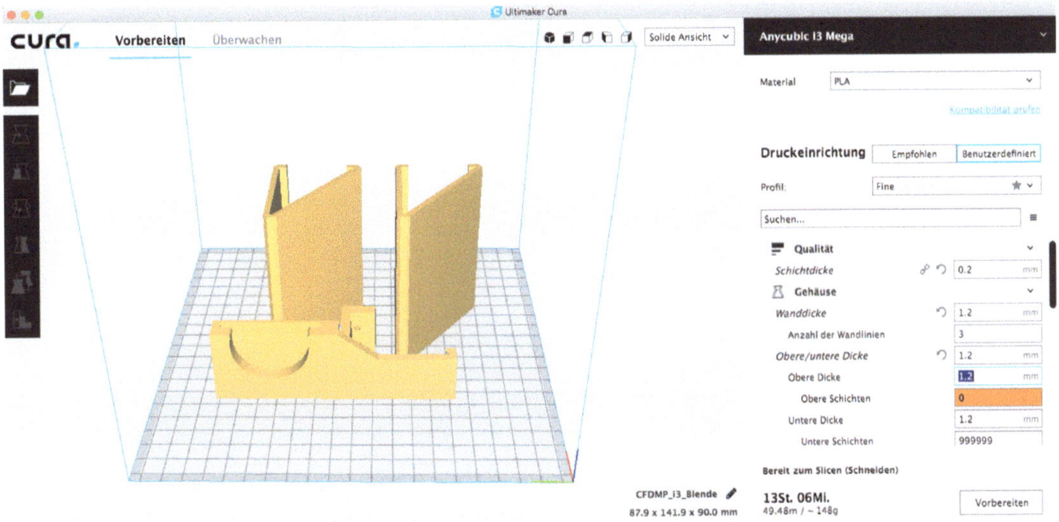

DXF EXPORT FOR CNC MILLING

When exporting DXF-files from a 2D model for CNC milling the `$fn` variable is essential for round shapes. In the example below, you see how the small holes look almost perfectly round in contrast to the much bigger half-circle cutout.

To recapitulate `$fn` stand for face-number and that is the maximum number of straight lines which will be used to draw a shape. The low amount of `24` in that example work for estimating the small drill-holes but it's to less for the big cutout. Before exporting the DXF-file you need to set `$fn` to a value which works good for the model - not to high that the CNC-router can handle it anymore and not to low to get nice round shapes!

To export a file render it first with the `F6`-key or use the command `Design -> Render`. Then click on `File` -> `Export` -> `DXF export...`

For so-called 2.5D milling, you can use DXF-file and for 3D milling use STL-files. `$fn` is equally important both cases - no matter if you export for milling or 3D printing.

LEARN FROM OTHERS

Painters and photographers learn to work with the light by studying the works of old masters. Programmers learn from open source projects how more experienced developers approach and solve a problem.

Josef Prusa, the developer of the very famous Prusa 3D printers, has published components of his printer as OpenSCAD files under

```
https://github.com/josefprusa
```

For example, open "`Prusa3-vanilla`" and within this folder the subfolder "`src`".

Take a closer look at these files and learn how parts can be created. The selection ranges from simple parts such as in the `belt-guide.scad` file to complex parts such as in the `extruder-block-slim.scad` file.

There is a lot to learn from looking through the files and analyzing them with the help of the modifiers.

LITTLE HELPERS

Use an alternative editor

Programmers often have an almost religious relationship with their editors. And yes, you can of course use your favorite editor if you want to use OpenSCAD. You can hide the OpenSCAD editor via `View` -> `Hide editor`.

If you now select the menu item `Design` -> `Automatically reload and activate preview`, the preview will be regenerated every time the file is saved. So you don't always have to switch between OpenSCAD and the editor of your choice to see the result of the changes.

Work faster with complex models

However, this function is also very useful for another purpose - if you are working on a very complex model, it may well take several seconds or even a few minutes to generate the preview... By deactivating the before mentioned function (*regardless of whether If you are working with an external editor or the internal editor in OpenSCAD*) the preview will only be calculated if you give OpenSCAD the corresponding command.

Have a look inside the model

Often you don't want to see any surfaces to see more precisely what is going on inside the model ... With `View` -> `Grid Only` we can achieve exactly that. The grid model shows the result of the last rendering! Therefore the preview and the grid model can deviate from each other if you forget to render again.

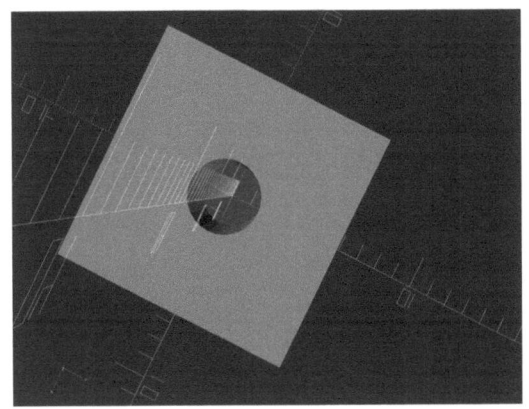 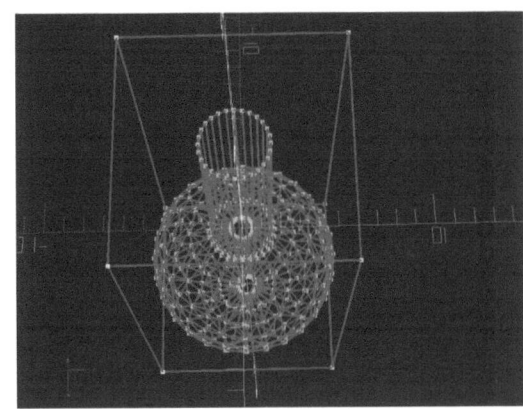

Even the view from above does not give an idea of what is going on in the model. Only the grid model reveals the sphere. In the next example, we don't see even with the grid view what is goind on... Only slicing the model in half provides a better insight into this improvised mold!

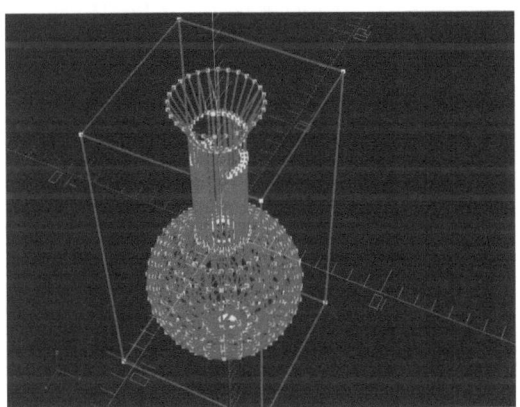 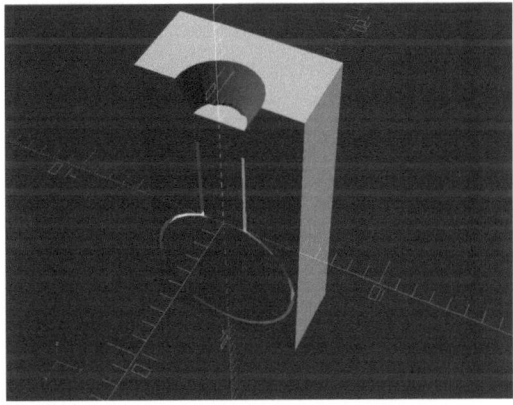

Since this function is not available at the push of a button, I used the following workaround:

First I created a module with the name `mold_form` and then I wrote this code:

```
difference(){
    mold_form();
    translate([0,-6,-11]) cube([6,12,25]);
}
```

Even if your model cannot or should not be flexible, it still makes sense to pack the whole model into one module for precisely these things. If you want to render the complete model, you only need to use the ! modifier...

```
difference(){
    !mold_form();
    translate([0,-6,-11]) cube([6,12,25]);
}
```

Remember, the ! and * Modifier also affect rendering ... Only # and % are limited to the preview. This allows you to switch between the section view and the full model with just a single character in the code.

MCAD - A OPENSCAD MODULE COLLECTION

The longer you work with OpenSCAD, the more modules, functions or other code snippets you will build yourself.

MCAD provides a collection of OpenSCAD code that allows you to add:

- modules for additional 2D and 3D shapes,
- modules for useful components such as ball bearings, screws, nuts, gears, ...
- useful constants and math functions
- etc.

to your projects with the use of the `include` command.

It's best to get an idea for yourself and take a look at the Github page of the project:
`https://github.com/SolidCode/MCAD`

BOOK RECOMMANDATIONS

People say assembly, the machine language, is a very difficult programming language. With this book, I want to show you that assembly is not that difficult at all. Assembly is different and doesn't work like modern high-level languages, but once you understand how to work with it, assembly becomes easy. This book provides a practical introduction to programming in assembly. Without torturing ourselves through the theoretical basics, we start right away and look at assembly and machine commands using practical examples. We will further highlight the stumbling blocks and challenges with low-level programming.

16,95 USD, ISBN: 979-8555204431

Python is an easy to learn, yet very diverse and powerful programming language and that for the language of choice for many hackers. Developing your own tools will give you a much deeper understanding of how and why attacks work.

After a short introduction to programming with Python, you will learn to write a wide variety of hacking tools using many practical examples. By integrating existing tools such as Metasploit and Nmap, scripts become even more efficient and shorter.

19,99 EUR, ISBN: 978-3752686159